Careers Working with Horses

Monty Mortimer

Kogan Page

First published 1983 by Kogan Page Limited
120 Pentonville Road, London N1 9JN

Copyright © Kogan Page 1983

British Library Cataloguing in Publication Data
Mortimer, Monty
    Careers working with horses.— (Kogan Page
    careers series)
    1. Horses   2. Horsemanship—Vocational guidance
    I. Title
    636.1'0023   SF309

    ISBN 0-85038-639-X (Hb)
    ISBN 0-85038-640-3 (Pb)

Printed in Great Britain by
The Anchor Press Ltd
Tiptree, Essex

Contents

Introduction

Introduction

Riding as a competitive sport, a serious hobby, or just a relaxing pastime has risen in popularity enormously in Great Britain over the past 10 to 20 years. This is perhaps due to the very wide coverage of show jumping and horse trials on television, and the attention that has been drawn to the sport by the enthusiasm of the Royal Family for racing, horse trials, show jumping, polo, and hunting.

It is estimated that over two million people ride regularly in the British Isles. By regularly is meant, more than once a week. Only a small percentage of these riders own their own horses. Many riders attend riding schools or hacking stables where horses are provided for them.

There are over 3000 licensed riding schools in Great Britain, 450 of which are approved by the British Horse Society.

The horse population is impossible to estimate but it is obvious that there are very many more horses and ponies used for leisure pursuits than ever there were before. Not only are they seen in the country areas, but also in large numbers in urban areas, and on patches of grass in and around the major towns and cities.

This continuing increase in horse popularity must be reflected in job opportunities in the horse world; not only those involving direct contact with horses but in all the peripheral activities; saddlery, the provision of riding clothes, the supplying of horse feeds, veterinary care, farriery, the building of stables, and the provision of horse transport, etc.

Young people are often attracted to employment with horses by the apparent glamour of the life and the sport of riding — the red coats and white breeches jumping large coloured fences at Wembly, or dashing event riders riding fast across country at Badminton or at an International Horse Trial. Unfortunately only a very few have the skill, facilities, or good fortune to reach these standards.

Most work connected with horses is physically hard work, often carried out very early in the morning under cold, wet conditions, winter and summer alike. Very little of it is in shining boots on a beautiful horse in front of a crowd of people. The hours are long, the work is hard, and the pay is usually modest. However, many people enjoy a full, happy, rewarding life working with horses and most of them would not think of doing anything else. Caring for horses is a demanding occupation. Those so employed must be physically fit and strong. Grooming a horse properly requires not only skill but strength and stamina. Much of the work concerned with looking after horses requires a good deal of physical strength. A bale of hay weighs about 50 pounds and there are usually plenty of these to be carried.

This does not mean that all people working with horses have to be giants with blacksmiths' muscles. Many small, even frail people are very successful horsemasters and stable managers. It is more a mental robustness that is required, the ability to find a way to cope, a sense of humour, and a determination to succeed. Working with horses is a way of life not just a job. In this sense it is very much more like farming, nursing, or being a musician. You do it because you really want to not just to earn your living.

To avoid disappointment and disillusion you should consider working with horses as a job to be done just about 24 hours a day. Then, any time you have off can be considered as a bonus. It is not possible to work with horses from nine till five, as some emergency or difficulty is always arising which demands your attention. However, in an efficiently run stable these are kept to a minimum and one is able to organise off duty life satisfactorily.

Pay for grooms is usually equated to the national basic agricultural wage which is watched over by the various agricultural trade unions. The National Association of Grooms is a developing organisation whose purpose is to look after the interests of grooms as regards pay, working hours, terms of employment, etc.

Pay for instructors is not so well organised, although the British Horse Society does from time to time issue guidelines on pay for those who hold its various teaching qualifications. The fees that an instructor can charge will depend on his qualifications, experience, and past success rate in his particular field.

To give yourself the best possible chance of a successful career with horses you should have at least a second 'string to your bow'. First it is important to complete your education at school. The subjects that you take will not necessarily be of use to you in your work, but it is an indication to a potential employer that you have the ability to be trained and to learn. It is a sign that you have the self discipline to set yourself standards, and the ability to achieve them.

In any career some knowledge of business management is essential. The ability to run a small office, to type, to do simple book keeping, or a knowledge of home economics will be an asset to you. You must at least be able to answer the telephone, write a business letter, and deal competently with customers and other members of the public.

How to Find Employment Working with Horses

First of all be sure that this is what you really want to do. You can do this by taking part in a work experience scheme, or by asking if you can help part time at your local riding school for experience, or by going on a course for a few weeks to get first hand experience of what is entailed in working with horses. This last option will however involve you in some expense.

Once you have decided that a life with horses is what

9

you really want, the next thing to decide is how you are going to train for this work, and what area particularly interests you.

To start with there are two basic courses open: to be a groom or an instructor. There is little chance of a career as a competition rider unless you are particularly talented. Even then, someone has to recognise your talents, find horses for you, and finance you until your reputation is established. So unless you have a good deal of money behind you, a career as a rider is probably out of your reach.

Areas of Work Available

For grooms: hunting stables, polo stables, racing stables, livery stables, riding schools, competition yards, and trade concerns that use heavy horses.

For instructors: riding schools, riding clubs, and pony clubs.

The Services: the Army and some Police Forces have mounted elements that require recruits from time to time.

Most employers will require trained personnel but some do provide 'in post' training. The thing to remember is that pay will be very low whilst one is in employment and still undergoing training.

This book is written to explain the areas of the horse world in which employment can be found, to give advice on how to get training to prepare yourself for work in a particular field, and to point out some of the difficulties and pitfalls that may be encountered along the way.

Part 1

Chapter 1
Riding Instructors

Introduction

The profession of riding instructor is an ancient and respected one. Certainly since 300BC when Xenophon wrote his first work on training horses and riders, this profession has played a part in the development of sport, art, military tactics, and the welfare of the horse.

To become a riding instructor requires the careful study of several techniques and subjects. With this in mind the British Horse Society administers and controls a progressive series of riding instructor qualifications which are second to none in the world. They are sought after by many foreign students as their excellence is accepted internationally.

These qualifications lead on gradually and logically from the very basic, fundamental studies of the subject at British Horse Society assistant instructor level to the intermediate instructor and instructor qualification and on to the fellowship of the British Horse Society, the highest qualification.

Assistant Instructor's Examination

The British Horse Society assistant instructor's examination is divided into two parts:

1. Preliminary teaching certificate.
2. The certificate of horsemastership.

Each part is taken separately.

The preliminary teaching certificate is to test the candidates' powers as instructors and the horsemaster's certificate tests the candidates' knowledge and ability as riders and horsemasters. Full details of these examinations can be obtained from:

> The British Horse Society, Examinations Office, British Equestrian Centre, Kenilworth, Warwickshire CV8 2LR.

Candidates for the British Horse Society assistant instructor's examination must:

1. Be over 17½ years of age.
2. Be members of the British Horse Society.
3. Hold four GCEs at O level (or their equivalent), one of which must be in an English language subject.

(After 20 years of age the O level requirement is no longer necessary.)

These examinations are constantly under review by the Society to ensure that they keep up with current trends and requirements. This may mean that from time to time changes are made to the various syllabuses. It is therefore very important that potential candidates should apply to the British Horse Society for up to date information.

A holder of the British Horse Society assistant instructor's certificate is *not* a complete trainer of horse and rider, and horsemaster. The qualification is simply an indication that he or she has studied the subject seriously at a basic level and has satisfied the examiners that he or she is capable of teaching, riding, and looking after horses at a basic level *under supervision*.

Intermediate Instructor's Examination

After about two years' practical experience as a BHSAI one should be seriously considering the next stage. This is the examination for the British Horse Society intermediate instructor's certificate. It is open to holders of the BHSAI certificate and there is no minimum age limit. It is obtained by passing *both* the BHS intermediate teaching certificate and any one of the following:

1. The BHS horse knowledge and riding certificate stage IV.
2. The Riding Club grade IV certificate.
3. The Pony Club A test certificate.

There are no age limits for this examination.

The examination requires a degree of maturity from the candidate showing some experience in the profession. The standard is half-way between the BHSAI and the British Horse Society instructor's (BHSI) examinations.

Holders of the BHS intermediate instructor's certificate can, at the age of 22, go on to take the British Horse Society instructor's certificate. This is taken in three parts:

1. The BHS equitation certificate.
2. The BHS teaching certificate.
3. The BHS stable manager's certificate.

This examination is for the mature, experienced instructor who can ride and instruct to a high standard. It is an advanced examination which requires a candidate to have experience as an instructor, and, in addition, all round ability as a rider.

Training

How does one train for these examinations? There are a number of ways, each with its own advantages and disadvantages.

1. At a riding school that runs courses to train students for a particular examination. The courses can be as short as three months or as long as a year. They are all well run and geared to getting candidates through the exam, the pass rate is high. The fees however are high too and one is unlikely to get a discretionary grant from the local council for this training. However grants are sometimes made, and application should be made direct to the local education authority.

2. As a working pupil at a riding school that offers this

facility. This is the most economical way to train, and under this arrangement the working pupil usually pays for accommodation and keep and in return for the work that she does in the stable yard she receives training for her examination. Many students are trained in this way and the success rate is high.

Before entering into a working pupil agreement, the potential working pupil, her parent or guardian should agree a contract in writing with the proprietor of the riding school providing the course. This contract may also be approved by the family solicitor. No reasonable riding school proprietor will refuse this.

It is recommended that the following points are covered in this contract.

☐ A broad description of the duties that the working pupil will be expected to carry out.
☐ Hours of work.
☐ Time off to include weekends.
☐ Arrangements for public holidays.
☐ Other holidays.
☐ The training that the working pupil will receive, both mounted and dismounted.
☐ The examination for which the working pupil will be trained, and the approximate date of the examination.
☐ Who will make the entry for the examination.
☐ Accommodation, to include bedding and linen etc.
☐ Provision of meals.
☐ Keep of working pupil's horse, if any.
☐ Taking part in competitions, if any.
☐ Hunting, if any.
☐ Practical teaching experience.
☐ All financial arrangements.
☐ Working clothes and equipment to be provided, and by whom.
☐ Period of probation.
☐ Any rules of discipline with regard to the pupil's conduct, eg dress, hair styles, make-up, time-keeping etc.

3. It is of course possible to train oneself for these

examinations. The syllabus can be obtained from the British Horse Society together with the recommended reading list. It is then necessary to find sufficient horses to ride and jump and a stable yard in which to work, if only part time, to obtain the necessary practical experience. It is also necessary to find someone to help you who has a knowledge of the riding standards required for the examination, otherwise you may be heading for an expensive disappointment.

The disadvantages of this method of preparation are obvious, but it has been done and if you cannot afford any sort of formal training and you have sufficient determination this can prove a successful way to train.

Where to Train

Having decided which method of preparation to follow, how do you find out where to train?

Read the weekly magazine *Horse and Hound* which is published on Fridays. This publication advertises schools and private individuals who run preparatory courses for BHS examinations, or who take working pupils preparing for these examinations. The schools that run these courses efficiently will, on application, send you a brochure, and you should write to the private individuals in accordance with the terms of the advertisement.

There are several riding schools that offer these courses so it is worth writing for a number of brochures and visiting a number of schools before you decide where you would like to train. You will of course be required to attend for an interview. It is often an advantage to attend these interviews with one or both of your parents if this is possible.

When you attend for your interview, as well as seeing the stables, horses and riding school, ask to see the student accommodation, bathrooms, dining room, and kitchen. This may save disappointment later.

Residential students should ask to see the training programme, and potential working pupils should ask to see the contract for working pupils. If a contract does not exist, then one *must* be drawn up.

One of the most important things to discuss at the interview is the exam you are being trained for, the date of the exam, and who will make the entry.

If you cannot find a suitable school at which to train in the advertisement columns of the *Horse and Hound*, the British Horse Society booklet 'Where to Ride' lists all the BHS approved schools in the British Isles with details of the training facilities that they offer.

Where to Find Work

Having passed the British Horse Society assistant instructor's examination, where does one find employment with horses? With this qualification you can be employed as a junior instructor or as a groom.

Most busy riding schools employ two, three or even more BHSAIs. They are employed to take novice riders, both children and adults, and usually have two or three horses or ponies to look after as well. Many riding schools provide in post training for their staff so helping to prepare them for the next step up the instructor's ladder.

Some competition yards, training show jumpers or eventers, employ BHSAIs as grooms, as the owners can be fairly sure that the holder of this qualification has had some basic training and has reached an acceptable standard.

Private family stables, that have perhaps a couple of hunters and ponies, often employ a BHSAI in preference to a groom, particularly where there are children to be taught. They quite often live in as part of the family and share in other household chores.

Positions for BHSAIs are regularly offered in the *Horse and Hound*, there are also some agencies who deal solely in stable staff and instructors. It is quite inexpensive to draft your own advertisement, giving your details, qualifications and interests, and to put it in the 'Situations Wanted' column in the *Horse and Hound*. This may well produce the required response.

When applying for any job, set about it in a businesslike way, write a formal application and have a neatly laid out curriculum vitae typed and ready to send to a potential employer. It is useful to have several copies of this ready to send.

When you accept a job remember that the law requires that you should be given a 'job description' (notes on what the job entails) and within 13 weeks of taking up the post you must be given a contract, preferably in writing.

Whether you intend to take further examinations or not it is important that you should continue your studies whilst you are working. As a busy instructor your own riding standards may fall and you may get into bad teaching habits whilst working on your own. You owe it to yourself as well as to your pupils to continue your studies and to take a refresher course from time to time.

Case Studies

Jill is 19 and is a *working pupil* at a large riding school in Warwickshire.

> I was very lucky in that I had a pony since I was seven years old and I always knew that I wanted to work with horses. I was a member of the Pony Club and I passed my C plus certificate. I got four O levels and did not want to go on at school as I was so keen to get on with my riding. My parents were not very keen on the idea of me working full time with horses at first, but it has all gone so well that I think that they are really quite pleased now.
>
> The working pupil course is a one-year course and is designed to train you for the British Horse Society assistant instructor's certificate. I have to pay £20 a week for my room and board and in exchange for the work that I do in the yard the school trains me for my exam. I get one riding lesson in a class of six students five days a week, and one classroom lesson on weekdays, these lessons are for about an hour or so. Of course all the other work that I do in the stable yard is training for my exam, we will be examined in grooming, handling and leading horses, saddling up, mucking out, and so on.
>
> The boss is very strict but I think that is important in a school like this. If we have long hair it always has to be tied back or in a hair net. We are not allowed to wear make-up in the yard or while we are riding, jewellery, particularly ear rings, is not allowed.
>
> The accommodation is quite good, I share a fairly big

17

room with one other girl who is on the course with me, and fortunately we get on really well together. The food is quite good too, rather stodgy and I tend to eat too much but we all get so hungry here.

Now I have been here six months I teach some of the children's classes which I really enjoy. This is all part of my training as I will have to take a class lesson as part of my exam.

My working day starts at 7 am when we all report for work in the yard. We muck out, water and feed the horses, and brush them down. We each have about three or four horses to do. At 8.30 am we go back for breakfast, and have to be changed into our riding clothes, saddled up, and back in the riding school for our lesson at 9 am. It's a bit of a rush, but then it's all a bit of a rush. We have a short break from 10 until 10.20 then I have my four horses to groom thoroughly, this takes up to two hours. After lunch I have to catch six ponies from the field as they are required for the local school children's lesson in the afternoon. The ponies have to be brushed down, have their feet picked out, and be saddled up ready for the children. I take this class sometimes which is quite a challenge.

The second half of the afternoon is when we usually get our classroom lesson. The subject is something in the BHSAI syllabus, feeding horses, veterinary care, general stable management, grooming, saddlery, or something of that sort. Sometimes we do a written paper on minor ailments in the horse.

We have a break for tea at about 4.30 pm and then back to the yard to bed down the horses, water and feed. Then comes the cleaning of all the tack that we have used that day, this takes an hour or so. Some of us will have an evening lesson to take. There is a roster for late night watering and checking the horses. This is done by two of us at our school at 10 pm. It is a bit of a tie but it is very important.

The school is closed on Mondays and I get every other weekend off. There is a roster for Monday duties of course but you get a day off in lieu if you're lucky! We are each allowed two weeks' holiday during our year's course but it is very difficult to find time to take it. There always seems to be something more important.

Our chief instructor is a BHSI and a very good rider, he takes us sometimes but we usually have another very good girl instructor who is an intermediate working for her instructor's.

The school makes all the arrangements for my exam

with the BHS and we are going to take some mock exams before the big day.

We have some overseas students here who are good fun and we learn a bit from them. I really enjoy it here and secretly I hope to do well enough in my exam for the boss to offer me a job as a junior instructor. I hope so.

Sue is 18 and has had two *working pupil* positions.

I had been going to this stable since I was 13, at first helping with the ponies, grooming, tacking up, and sweeping the yard. I did this on Saturdays at first but it built up until I was spending all my spare time at the stables. My parents thought that it was a good thing as it gave me something to do. Sometimes I got a free ride which I really enjoyed. When I left school I had only two GCEs so I could not do my BHSAI as I had wanted to. I could take my BHS horsemaster's certificate though, and take the rest when I am over 20 and do not need the O levels.

I tried for a job at the stables but the owner said he could not afford to pay me a wage. He said that he would teach me to ride for my exam in exchange for working for him and that I could live in the caravan at the stables. This seemed a very good idea at the time and it all started well. I really enjoyed working full time with horses. The riding lessons that I got were very few and far between and I got no training on theory at all. I was looking after nine horses on my own and really never got a day off. My working day started at 6 am and finished at about 9 pm, later if the owner had been away at a show for the day. Nearly every weekend was taken up at the riding school with indoor show jumping competitions which went on sometimes until 10 pm.

I suppose it was all quite good fun but I was not being trained for my exam; I was doing very long hours for no pay and I felt that I was getting nowhere. Of course I realise now that it was partly my fault as I should have had a written contract with the stable owner before I started. But how was I to know that? I was only 16 and I don't think that I had ever heard of a contract.

At one of the show jumping competitions a lady rider offered me a job at her stables where she kept her show jumpers and trained three working pupils for their BHS exams. It was a much smaller yard than before, the owner was very strict and had very high standards. This shook me a bit at first but I soon got into the swing of it and I realise how much better it is. She keeps to a very strict timetable and everyone knows exactly where she stands. The best thing about it is that we have a written contract which lays out in detail what is expected from both parties. I take my horse-master's exam in two months' time and feel really confident now.

The working pupils here live in a cottage next to the stables and cook their own food which is provided by the owner. We work very hard and for long hours and do not get much time off. We do get £5 a week pocket money though which helps a bit.

Barbara is 19½ and has been employed for one year as an *assistant instructor* at a very busy riding school in Lancashire.

I passed my BHSAI at a big riding school in Yorkshire having been a working pupil there for a year. I could not possibly have been able to pay the fees as a student, they were nearly £100 a week, but I learnt just as much, perhaps even more, as a working pupil.

On completion of my course I went to America for three months to teach riding at a summer camp. This was really hard work and very poorly paid, but I learnt a great deal about looking after myself and dealing with difficult people in that three months. When I came back to England I took a short holiday and then I wrote off for three jobs that were advertised in the *Horse and Hound*. They all asked for 'an experienced BHSAI'. I was not very experienced but my stay in America had given me the confidence that I needed to apply for these jobs. Two of them were at riding schools and one was at a hunter and livery stables. I was interviewed for all three posts and to my surprise was offered all three. I turned down the hunter and livery yard because the standards maintained there did not appear to come up to the standards that I had been trained to expect. The two riding schools were very similar and about the same size. I chose this one because they do a lot of work with riding for the disabled which I am very interested in, and generally it seemed to have a happier atmosphere.

Now having been here for nearly a year I am very glad that I made this choice. My pay was put up a little after my first six months which was a probationary period and I have been promised a further increase if and when I pass my intermediate instructor's exam. I have just passed my BHS stage IV and I am due to take my intermediate in three weeks' time. I am a bit nervous about it but I have had lots of help from the chief instructor here, and fortunately there are two other girls who are a little ahead of me employed here who are taking the exam at the same time as me. This has helped me a lot.

I have my own room here which is next to the students' accommodation. It's small and a bit noisy but it is quite useful to be near the students as it helps me to keep an eye on what they are up to! I share a bathroom with three other members of the staff which is a bit inconvenient sometimes.

We all eat in the students' dining room and a charge for this and our accommodation is deducted from our pay.

I am responsible for what we call The Blue Yard which means that I have six riding school horses living in and four ponies living out to look after. I have two working pupils to help me do this and I am responsible for their practical training on the yard.

We all start work at 7 am when we muck out, water and feed, and brush off the horses' night stains. We probably catch up the ponies at this time too, and get them cleaned up ready for the children's rides.

At 8.15 am we go to breakfast and have to be back on the yard, dressed in riding clothes, ready to start work at 9 am. Sometimes I take the working pupils' ride on week-days but at the weekends I have four or five rides of pupils — children or adults — on both days.

Every day of the week the horses and ponies have to be watered, fed, groomed, and exercised in some way. Stables have to be mucked out, haynets filled, tack cleaned, and the yard always seems to need sweeping. So you see I have a really busy life. I am finished most evenings by about 6 pm unless I have an evening lesson or I have to supervise the working pupils who are on late night stable duty.

The school is closed on Mondays and only a skeleton staff is kept on to muck out, water and feed. I get every other weekend off and two weeks' paid holiday a year. This does seem like long hours but we are in the leisure industry which means that we must be prepared to work when our customers are at their leisure.

I get quite a lot of riding and I enjoy my job very much, I don't think that I would change it for any other job that I know.

Alison is 20, a qualified *assistant instructor*, and works for a family who have two hunters and two children's ponies. They live in a large house with stables and a paddock in Buckinghamshire.

Having had a pony myself since I was nine I was lucky enough to have passed my Pony Club B test which I took when I was 15. I knew that I wanted to work with horses but my father insisted that I took some other qualification first. At school I sat and passed six O levels but I did not want to stay on to take A levels. So I left school and did a one-year secretarial course which included shorthand and typing, some other secretarial work, and book keeping. I am glad that I did it now, not that I use the shorthand and typing much, but the general education was good and I grew up a lot in that year between leaving school and starting my BHSAI training.

I did a three-month BHSAI preparation course at a riding school in Surrey. It was hard work and fairly expensive but it was a BHS approved school and the local education authority luckily gave me a grant to help towards my food and accommodation.

I met the lady I work for now when her hunter was at livery at the school at which I trained. When I got my AI she asked me if I would like to go and work for her, look after her two hunters, and teach her children to ride. That is how I came to be doing this job. I like it very much. I have two beautiful hunters to look after and exercise and I enjoy teaching the two children who are now beginning to take part in competitions, so I take them with their ponies in the landrover and trailer to the local horse shows and pony club events.

I have my own room in a very nice house and I am very well looked after. My pay is small but I get a lot 'in kind'.

The only problem is that I am not getting anywhere with my own riding, and I am not getting the training that I need to enable me to take my intermediate exam. I enjoy teaching the children but they are not at the standard that I need for the intermediate teaching. So if I want to make progress I will have to move on to a riding school or competition yard.

Richard is 24 he is a British Horse Society *instructor* and is at present living in Hertfordshire.

I left school at 16 with eight O levels and went to work at a local riding school where I was really just a labourer/groom. My main job was looking after riding school horses and ponies, getting them ready for rides. Whilst I was there I did get quite a lot of riding and, as it was a busy riding school, I learnt quite a lot from listening to the several qualified instructors that were employed there.

At 17½ I decided that I would like to take my BHS assistant instructor's examination. This is difficult to do without some financial backing, however I managed to persuade the school to take me on as a working pupil. That meant that I still continued to do my work but that I joined in with the course of students who were training for the BHSAI. During this time I was not paid, but as it was only for three months my parents were able to help out. I passed my exam and continued to work at the same school as a paid instructor. I say paid, that is a slight exaggeration. My pay was £30 a week for about a 60-hour week, but I did get free board and lodging and quite a lot of riding. During this time I was given several rides on clients' horses in show jumping, horse trials, and dressage competitions. This enabled me to get some competition experience which is so important to a riding instructor.

After two years of riding school teaching I took the BHS intermediate teaching certificate. This is for instructors who have some teaching experience and is half-way between the assistant instructor and the instructor's qualification. I was given quite a lot of help in preparation for this examination by our chief instructor so fortunately I passed. To get the full BHS intermediate instructor's certificate I also had to sit one of the BHS more advanced riding examinations and pass it. I sat what is called the BHS riding and horse knowledge certificate grade IV which I passed and so got the full qualification.

The next stage in the riding instructor's career is to pass the BHS instructor's certificate. This is the top examination and requires a lot of study and preparation.

It is a very difficult exam to prepare for because, not only do you have to ride horses at a fairly advanced level, but you also have to instruct riders at a fairly advanced level. Finding both horses and riders to practise on can be very difficult.

I was now 19½, and the riding school where I had been working since I left school had neither the horses nor the riders to train me up to I level, and I could not take the I exam until I was 22.

The obvious thing for me to do was to try to find a job somewhere where I could work as a rider/groom in a yard that trained either jumpers or dressage horses to an advanced level. I managed to get a place in a professional show jumping yard where I learnt a lot about training show jumpers and the general 'rough and tumble' of the show jumping world, which was all very new to me. It was hard work but I rode many very good horses that were all quite different to anything that I had ridden before.

After a year of this I decided to try to find work in a dressage yard so I answered an advertisement asking for a groom/trainee rider in a dressage stable in Austria. I had never been abroad before so this was all very much a new adventure to me. I spoke no German and the trainer spoke very little English but he had a way of making me understand what he meant. My stay in Austria was a real eye opener for me; I had no idea how demanding a rider could be or of the degree of training that was expected at an early age. I don't think that there is anywhere in England where I could have learnt so much in such a short period of time.

I came back to England age 21½ with my head full of very grand ideas, but I was soon brought back down to earth when I started work at a British riding school again. I studied hard for my I exam attending various short, two- or three-day courses on the subject. When I was 22½ I took the riding and the teaching parts of the exam which I passed. The stable management section requires rather more experience so I left it for one more year. With the extra preparation I was able to pass it the following year.

Now I have my full BHSI there is plenty of work for me to do, particularly riding clubs and pony clubs. I take one or two riding clubs regularly and train their teams for competitions. I do quite a lot of work with the pony clubs, teaching at two or three camps each summer. Most of all I like to train competition riders. The only way to get more pupils is to have success with those that you have got. Success breeds success.

I would like to have my own school sometime but that requires a large capital investment that I cannot raise, so I am content to be working freelance for the moment. I have tried to broaden my horizons by becoming a British Show Jumping Association judge, a British Horse Society dressage judge and I hope to get onto the British Horse Society list of examiners. Course building for show jumping competitions is also something that I am interested in but that will have to wait for later.

There are some difficulties involved in being a freelance instructor. First I am self employed this means that there are special regulations that apply regarding income tax and national insurance contributions. Second I need some sort of loss of earnings insurance; if I fall off a horse and break my leg I cannot earn my living. Then there is the question of how much should I charge. This depends entirely on one's experience and quality as an instructor. Travelling is very expensive so I have to make sure that my travelling expenses are included in my fee. I drive a car now, but it would be very useful for me to have a motorised caravan to work from. This would save a lot in accommodation charges and would be much more convenient.

I enjoy my work and I have been lucky in some ways. I have still got a long way to go and much studying to do before I can consider myself a top trainer.

Chapter 2

Grooms and Stable Managers

Introduction

For anyone who wants to be a competent groom, there is no substitute for experience. To work in a well run stable where one can have experience of handling many different horses, under many different circumstances, is the only way in which this vital experience can be obtained. However some formal training and study is very helpful, particularly now that science plays a much greater part in animal management, and rule of thumb principles although still very important are being supplemented and complimented by scientific study.

For this reason the various national horse bodies have their own examinations for grooms and stable managers.

They are as follows:

1. The British Horse Society
   (a) Certificate of horsemastership
   (b) Stable manager's certificate.
2. The Association of British Riding Schools
   (a) Groom's diploma.

It is strongly recommended that anyone who intends to earn his or her living as a professional groom should study for and take one or more of these examinations depending on the area of the horse world in which he or she intends to work.

A groom's duties cover every aspect of the day to day care of the horse. These duties include:

☐ Mucking out
☐ Grooming and strapping
☐ Feeding
☐ Cleaning tack and saddling up
☐ Exercising and leading, both mounted and dismounted
☐ Elementary veterinary care and sick nursing
☐ Preparation for and travelling with horses by road, sea and air
☐ Care of the horse when at grass.

In addition it is very useful for a groom to be able to drive and to hold a Heavy Goods Vehicle licence.

All grooms should be able to ride, not necessarily as experts but safely and competently at walk, trot, and canter. This is necessary as daily exercise is a vital part of the horse's well being. A well trained groom will be able to safely lunge a horse for exercise and will be able to ride one horse and lead another.

As is the case in all areas of the horse world, a groom should have a sound knowledge of riding and road safety together with a basic knowledge of human first aid. The British Horse Society issues comprehensive written information on both of these important subjects.

Formal Qualifications for Grooms

The British Horse Society Certificate of Horsemastership

Candidates, who must have reached the age of 17½, will be examined in the following:

Equitation
Stable management and horsemastership
Minor ailments, a 45 minute written paper
Lungeing, riding and leading.

EQUITATION, RIDING ON THE FLAT
In this phase of the examination the candidate is required to show that he or she has a good seat and position and the ability to apply the aids correctly. The candidate must

show a knowledge of the correct basic paces of the horse and the ability to ride simple school movements. This phase of the examination lasts 45 minutes. The examination will consist of a ride of about four or five candidates working as a class. An experienced instructor will take the class and give the commands throughout the ride. Each candidate will ride at least three horses and the work is done either in an indoor riding school or in an outdoor riding area.

JUMPING

In this phase candidates are required to jump a course of six to eight fences about three feet in height. This may be indoors or outside. It will be a simple, flowing course over a variety of fences including a double. The horses will be riding school type horses and all will be capable of jumping the course freely. They will probably all have been schooled round the course on the day before the examination. Candidates will be required to ride two horses each and will be given the opportunity of a warm up fence before they jump their rounds. The examiners will be looking at the candidate's position when jumping, suppleness, ability to keep the horse in balance between fences, approach to each fence, and ability to ride a smooth track at a good speed, maintaining impulsion.

STABLE MANAGEMENT AND HORSEMASTERSHIP

Practical stable management. In this phase candidates are required to carry out six or so practical stable management tasks in about 45 minutes. They are also asked to discuss the work that they have done and the equipment that they have used.

Some typical practical tasks would be:

1. To fit a horse's snaffle bridle, running martingale and general purpose saddle, and be prepared to discuss whether or not the tack fits him and is suitable for use.
2. To fit working bandages to a horse's legs, bearing in mind he is going out to do some fast, cross country

training. Discuss protecting the horse's legs for jumping.
3. To fit a poultice to a horse's foot to draw a puncture wound in the sole.

Practical/oral stable management. In this phase, which is again about 45 minutes, candidates are required to take part in group discussion to show their knowledge of clipping, shoeing, conformation, stable construction, and the horse in general. The discussion will be held in a loose box where a horse, horse shoes, farrier's tools, and clippers will be provided.

Some typical questions would be:

1. Describe the horse we have in the stable with us.
2. Is he sound?
3. Why do we shoe horses?
4. When and how often would you clip your horse?

Oral stable management. This phase is once again 45 minutes and is conducted as a discussion with about four or five candidates taking part. The examiner will require candidates to show a sound knowledge of how to look after a horse both in the stable and out at grass. The subjects covered will include, feeding the horse, stable routine, turning a horse out to grass, roughing off, bringing up from grass, preparing for a day's hunting, care of the horse after a day's hunting, etc.

In total, candidates are examined in stable management for about two hours.

THE MINOR AILMENTS WRITTEN PAPER

This 45 minute paper is designed to test the candidate's knowledge of, and ability to treat, the health problems most often encountered in running a stable. It is not a test of his ability to write English nor is it a veterinary examination. However, legible handwriting and clear, correct English are definitely helpful to the examiner who is marking the papers.

Some typical questions might be:

1. How can you tell when your horse is:
   Healthy?
   Not very well?
   Very ill?
2. Write short notes on:
   Azoturia.
   Lampas.
   Thrush.
3. How can colic be caused?
   How would you recognise it?
   How would you treat it?

LUNGEING, RIDING AND LEADING

Lungeing. Candidates are required to lunge a horse or pony for exercise only. A trained horse or pony will be provided for this phase; he will be fitted with a lunge cavesson and a lunge rein and boots. A lunge whip will also be provided. Candidates are required to show that they are safe to lunge a horse or pony, have a good knowledge of fitting the lunge tack, and can handle the lunge rein and whip competently. This phase lasts about ten minutes.

Riding and leading. Here candidates are required to show that they can effectively ride one horse and lead another in walk and trot on the road.

Successful candidates in this examination will be awarded the Brtish Horse Society certificate in horsemastership. Holders of this certificate are qualified to take the BHS horse knowledge and riding certificate stage IV and at the age of 22 years the BHS stable manager's certificate.

The BHS Stable Manager's Certificate

This is an advanced examination which includes showing sound, experienced knowledge in all aspects of horse care. For example feeding, exercise, conditioning for various types of work, fitness, health, practical veterinary knowledge, details to look for when buying, and detection and treatment of lameness.

Candidates must be familiar with all aspects of organising and running a yard, eg staffing, layout, stable construction, book keeping, buying fodder and other necessary equipment.

A sound, basic knowledge must be shown regarding the care of mares and foals and young stock, together with the care of grassland.

Candidates are required to give a five minute talk on a given subject.

The Association of British Riding Schools Groom's Diploma

This examination is open to candidates aged 18 years and over. It is with very little exception a practical examination held over one and a half days starting at 2 pm on the first day and finishing at about 4.30 pm on the second day. Full details can be obtained from the general secretary, (see p. 95). Please send a stamped, addressed envelope and 25p for a copy of the syllabus.

The diploma is intended to provide a guide for employers in the selection of competent grooms who are capable of working on their own. The assistant groom's certificate will be awarded to candidates who fall just below diploma standard. This certificate is an indication that the holder is capable of being employed as a groom under supervision. In this examination honours are awarded to candidates who attain an exceptionally high standard of competence.

The examination will cover the care of the fit stabled horse. Candidates will be expected to show a high standard of overall knowledge and be able to apply that knowledge to specialised areas; competition horses, polo ponies, show horses, and ponies, etc.

Candidates will be required to demonstrate their knowledge of, and their ability in the following:

Daily stable routine
Saddlery
Shoeing
Feeding
Veterinary care of the horse
Riding
Lungeing

Management of grass and stables
Administration of a stable yard.

The candidate's general efficiency will also be taken into consideration regarding the handling of horses, tidiness and economy.

The National Association of Grooms

This Association works actively and effectively on behalf of those who have embarked on careers with horses outside the racing industry.

Currently the Association is working towards a minimum wage, and agreed allowances for board and lodging based on the Agricultural Wages Board rates. This will cover everyone working with horses in all types of establishment be they concerned with eventers, show jumpers, hunters, polo ponies, driving, heavy horses, showing, studs, livery yards, private, and riding stables.

One of the main aims of the Association is to establish a National Apprentice Training Scheme similar to that run by the Agricultural Training Board, whereby only establishments with adequate facilities and instructional training staff can qualify to accept trainees. Training will be closely monitored and trainees will receive an accepted minimum wage, the employer being subsidised from a central body for part of this.

The National Association of Grooms is registered as a trade union but is very much opposed to any kind of aggressive action to achieve its aims.

Full details of this Association can be obtained from the secretary, (see p. 95).

Case Studies

John is 20 and is employed as a *groom* by a show jumping rider and trainer who has a stable yard just outside Birmingham.

When I was at school in Birmingham I always wanted to be in the countryside and I never much liked being in the big city. I particularly liked being with animals and really wanted to work on a farm when I left school. The Job Centre in

Birmingham found me a job on a farm where I worked for just over a year. I learned to drive the tractor there and did general farm work. The farmer and his daughters had horses, show jumpers mainly, and I helped out in the stables and got really interested in it all. Most of my spare time I spent going to shows with them, where I learnt a lot both about horses and working as a groom at a show. It was hard work with a lot of travelling involved in getting to the shows.

At one big show I happened to mention that I would like to work full time as a groom looking after show jumpers and I was introduced to the man that I work for now. He said that he was looking for a good groom to travel with his horses to all the shows and offered me the job on a month's trial, I have now been with him for just over a year.

I look after three horses completely, that means mucking out, watering, feeding, grooming, exercising, and tack cleaning. I also have to get the horses ready when they are required for work or to go to a show.

My day starts at 6.30 am when I muck out, water, and feed. Then if the owner is going to school them, I have to get the horses ready for whenever he wants them. This is usually sometime during the morning. I have to be there, to move or put up the show jumps as he requires them.

Then during the rest of the day I water and feed the horses three or four times and groom all three, which is very important and quite hard work.

The outdoor jumping season is from about April to September, then from October to March we are very busy with the indoor jumping circuits.

We average about one show a week during the year, sometimes more. We are often away for three or even four days. The horse box is very big and has good accommodation for the grooms, sometimes sleeping accommodation is provided for grooms at a really big show.

I can ride well enough to exercise some of the horses and I would like to learn more about the jumping side but that is all in the future.

One thing that I would tell anyone who was thinking of being a groom is that if you are interested in time off or regular hours or making a lot of money then forget about working as a groom. But if you want a really varied life with a lot of travel, excitement, and the opportunity to meet people this is a very rewarding job.

I get about £70 a week but I do not have many expenses. I take a day off when I can and I usually work about a ten-hour day, longer sometimes when we are travelling to a show or we have a class to jump in the evening. I enjoy it very much and I wouldn't change it.

Jill is 20 and she lives in Dorset where she is employed as a *groom* in a private hunting yard.

I have been working with horses and ponies for as long as I can remember. When I was very small we lived by the seaside where I used to help with the donkeys and ponies on the beach. Then when we moved away I helped out at weekends and in the holidays at a local livery stable. When I left school I got a job at a riding school, looking after the ponies that were kept out at grass. I really wanted to do more than this so I looked around for a job where I could work with hunters or competition horses. I was 17 then and no one wanted me as I had no experience of fit horses kept in the stable rather than out at grass. What I really needed to do was to get one of the groom's certificates. I could not do the BHSAI because I did not have the O levels. The riding school knew me and said that they would take me on as a working pupil to train for the BHS horsemaster's certificate. They would accommodate me and give me a little pocket money. It worked out very well and in six months I passed my exam.

I got my present job from an advertisement in the local paper. A lady wanted a groom to look after two hunters and help in a small horse dealing business. Now I have two hunters to look after and perhaps up to five young horses that are in the yard waiting to be sold. I get a lot of riding with the hunters to exercise and quite a lot of young horses to work. In the hunting season it is a bit hectic, they hunt about three days a fortnight which takes quite a lot of preparation and cleaning up afterwards. The work I like most is buying in the new horses and getting them going well enough to sell on. Some are grown horses that perhaps have a problem that we have to try to sort out, and some are young and just have to be taught basic good manners etc so that they can be safely sold on.

I have a nice room to myself and with all found I get £40 a week. It's not much, as I do quite long hours and do not get much time off. I do get the use of the landrover though when I need to go into town so that saves me the expense of running a car.

David is 20 years old and he lives in Kent. He left school aged 18 having gained two A levels in maths and biology. He now works as a *groom* in a point to point yard.

I have always wanted to work with horses and have never really considered anything else. I think that I could have got into university or college with my A level passes but that was not what I wanted to do. I have been riding since I was six years old, I started riding on my cousin's pony. We had no instruction, I suppose we learnt by trial and error. At 12 years old I got my first pony and at 14 I joined the Pony Club. Each summer I went to Pony Club camp and I attended all the rallies. I owe so much to the Pony Club. I am sure that I would not have the job that I have today if it were not for the training I got in the Pony Club.

My present job was advertised in the local paper. I applied for it, was interviewed and got it. I have now been doing it for nearly two years. The yard I work in is a point to point yard. That is, genuine hunters that also race. They have to be hunted a certain number of days each year to qualify to run in a point to point.

There are two of us working here, I am the junior and there is a head lad who is quite a bit older than me. We do about two or three horses each. The number varies but there are usually five or six horses in. The job consists of looking after the horses in all respects. We are not watched over very much but very high standards are expected. Our yard is so well run and the equipment so good that I think that it has spoilt me for anywhere else.

We start at 7 am I muck out all three, feed two, and ride one. When I get back I feed him and work one of the other two. After this I usually have a cup of tea or a light late breakfast and go to ride the third one. This usually takes me up until about 11.30. I then groom all three, this takes between 30 and 45 minutes per horse. They are then watered and fed and we go for lunch about 1.30 pm. The afternoon is taken up tack cleaning, collecting forage, doing repairs, and general maintenance. About 4.30 pm we bed down, water and feed. The horses all have to be checked at about 10.30 pm when we fill up the water buckets, straighten up the rugs, and put the night hay nets in.

On a racing day it is rather different. We start perhaps at 5.30 am to get those that are not going racing exercised, and then we have to get those who are going ready to travel. This takes quite a lot of preparation bandaging legs, putting on rugs and guards of various sorts to protect them on the journey. It is very important to make sure that you have all the tack and equipment required for the race. It is part of my job to ensure that it all gets there on time and in good condition.

We have a small horse box that will take three horses. It is below the weight when you have to hold an HGV licence to drive it so that means that I am usually the driver as well.

The race days are the real excitement. It is always good when your horses win or even do well. A lot depends on the jockey — some are very good — some not so good. I have had one ride in a point to point and I hope to get more. The real perk of this job is that we hunt all the horses between the two of us which gives us a lot of sport in the winter.

I don't really take any holidays and we take it in turns to have Sundays off. The summer is slack as the horses are out at grass, so I could take some time off if I wanted to. In the winter we are very busy, some weeks I do up to 80 hours, and I suppose I average about 70 hours a week in the hunting season. You can expect that if you want to work with horses.

My accommodation is a mobile home which is very comfortable and my fuel and light are all paid for, I provide my own food.

The pay is terrible — I get £40 a week, but I don't need much money at present. When I do need more I shall have to do something about it. My ambition is to have a yard of my own and to train a few point to pointers but that is all in the future. At present I am enjoying myself and learning a lot so I am really very happy with my lot.

Chapter 3

Racing

Stablehands and Apprentice Jockeys

It's one thing to get a job in a racing stable, but it's quite another thing to actually get a ride on a racecourse. Only a tiny fraction of apprentices get even a single ride in public. Most would-be jockeys remain stablehands and perhaps go on to become head lads (this is a job title which applies to both boys and girls).

Being an apprentice jockey means learning the hard way. You start as a stablehand and for the first few weeks you do nothing but help one of the experienced stablehands with the labouring — mucking out, fetching straw, filling haynets, sweeping the yard, changing the horses' water, and so on. This arrangement has its advantages though. It gives you the chance to get used to this rather special way of life. For example, if you have moved away from home you have new surroundings to get to know. Even if you are working at a local stable you usually have to live in a hostel on site. In these, there may be rules governing smoking, and drinking alcohol on the premises. Sometimes a colour television and other amenities are provided, but however good facilities are, not everyone can take the life at a racing stable. Anyway, if after the first weeks you still want to go into racing, you will probably stay the course. There is a National Joint Council for stable staff which lays down terms and conditions of employment (including a minimum wage level) to which all stable staff over 19 years of age (18 in Newmarket) are entitled after one year's service.

When the trainer or the head lad is satisfied that you are

a responsible type suitable for looking after horses and that you will fit in with the rest of the people at the stable, you get a couple of horses to look after. This is one of the best moments of your early career. The horses you 'do', though at first 'old uns' rather than next year's Derby winner, rapidly seem to become as much yours as if you owned them yourself.

Looking after horses is hard work. As an apprentice jockey you are responsible for mucking out, grooming, feeding, and exercising your two or three. You are up at dawn, if not before, in winter and summer, rain and shine, getting the horse which is in 'first lot' ready for exercise. First you put the head collar on the horse and tie it up. Then you muck out the stable — which must be done very thoroughly if the horses are to remain healthy — and carry the muck in a sack to the muck heap. On the return journey you collect some fresh straw to put down. After this you brush the horse till the coat shines and saddle it. Then you ride the horse out to the 'gallops' — the stretch of open country where the exercise takes place. For this you wear jodhpurs and a crash helmet.

When you get back from the ride you take off the bridle, saddle, and rug and give the horse a rub down with a damp swab to clean off the sweat. You have to be particularly careful with the areas covered by the saddle and girth, which can rub and cause a sore place or 'gaul'. Mud must be cleaned off the horse's legs with a handful of straw or with a sponge and a bucket of water, and lastly you must carefully take out any stones from the horse's feet that he may have picked up. This is vital or the horse can go lame. Before you have your own breakfast, you feed your horses. You have to watch continually for the slightest sign of illness or injury.

You usually have your breakfast after 'first lot', (you may have to pay towards your board and lodging). After breakfast you groom and ride your second horse in 'second lot' and perhaps do a third lot or more. When this is done it is time for cleaning the tack — the saddles and bridles etc, which takes until lunchtime. From lunch time until 4 pm or so you are free. Then the horses are again groomed and fed before being inspected by the trainer and head lad. At this grooming you give special attention to brushing and trimming the manes and tails, sponging the eyes and nose, checking for foot troubles and oiling the feet. After supper the apprentices are free again until bedtime. A precise time is not usually specified, but it cannot be very late if you are to get up at the early hour which the job demands.

On the day of a race you go with your horse in the horse box, taking tools and brushes with you. When you get to the course, your first job is grooming. Just before the race you walk the horse round to get any stiffness out of his legs after the journey and help him to get used to the surroundings. Some horses are particularly nervous at this stage and start to play up, so you need to be ready to calm them down. After he has been saddled you walk him around the parade ring in front of the public before the jockey mounts and canters to the start. It may be a bit frustrating at first to see someone else mount and walk 'your' horse out onto the course, but you have the consolation of knowing that one day it could be you in the saddle. And if 'your' horse wins you have the honour of leading him into the winners' enclosure.

Although there are no specific educational qualifications necessary, it will certainly do no harm to have reached a reasonable standard. The 1977 leading apprentice, Jimmy Bleasdale, had four O levels, and the 1980 leading apprentice had six CSEs. Riding experience is useful, though you need not necessarily have been to a riding school. Most trainers prefer you to start serious riding training with them.

Horses can be nervous and you must be able to move among them calmly and quietly so as not to unsettle them.

However, there is one qualification that you simply must have — the right physique. On leaving school you should weigh less than six and a half stones. The weight for qualified flat race jockeys is between seven and about nine stones. A main reason, in fact, that so many apprentices fail to become jockeys is that they grow too heavy.

How to Find Work

It is possible to get a job by having your name forwarded by *your* careers officer to the National Trainers Federation via the Reading Careers Office, Fourth Floor, 7 Cheapside, Reading RG1 7PX. The Federation circulates your details to racing stables in England, Wales, and Scotland. Trainers then get in touch with you direct. In 1980, 70 applied in this way 40 boys and 30 girls. The applications which were then circulated produced the following results: 25 started work with a trainer — 20 boys and five girls. Four boys were discharged after trials, and one has been recommended for a Goodwood course. The rest are still employed by trainers. All those successful had some worthwhile riding experience before applying for this.

It is proposed in the very near future to set up a new apprentice training scheme in a permanent training school. It is intended that the school should provide training at two levels: basic courses up to the level of exercising thoroughbreds — for stable staff, and advanced courses for potential work riders and potential flat and jump jockeys. The basic course will probably be open to both school leavers and those already in working yards. The advanced course will be restricted to those who have proved themselves on the basic course and/or in a stable yard. There will be no set academic requirements, but size, weight, and a willingness to learn will be important. Further information may be obtained from: The Careers and Occupational Information Centre, The Manpower Services Commission, Moorfoot, Sheffield SW1 4PQ, tel 0742 753275. Please remember to send a stamped and addressed envelope with your inquiry.

Apprentice Jockey Courses, Goodwood, Sussex

Six courses are run each year, and each course is for seven weeks. They are full-time residential courses, held at Goodwood House, close to the famous racecourse.

Pupils are taught to:

1. Ride.
2. Look after a horse.
3. Carry out elementary stable management.

Entry qualifications:

1. Both boys and girls are accepted for training.
2. Apprentices must come straight from school at 16, or only a little over.
3. Boys must weigh under seven stones, girls up to eight stones.
4. Successfully attend an interview at which the candidate must produce a letter from his/her headmaster stating that he/she is of average intelligence. A candidate must also state whether or not he/she has any convictions by a juvenile court.

Applications should *not* be made earlier than six to nine months before leaving school. Young people wishing to take this course should find out as much as possible about working with racehorses before they decide to apply. A complete list of racehorse trainers in England, Scotland, and Wales can be found at your local reference library in a book called *Horses in Training*. It would be very much to your advantage to write to a local trainer asking him if you could visit his stable, or perhaps work part time for him, to find out whether or not you really do want to work with racehorses. All applicants should have some riding experience. For further details and an application form write to: The Apprentices' School, Goodwood Stables, Chichester, Sussex PO18 0PX. There is no charge for this course, it is financed by The Horserace Betting and Levy Board.

National Hunt Racing

As well as flat racing there is also National Hunt racing. This includes steeplechasing and hurdle racing. Entry into this field is similar to that of flat racing, and some trainers train both flat racehorses and steeplechasers, but this is the exception rather than the rule. One advantage here is that there is a little more leeway as regards the jockey's weight, as National Hunt horses usually carry more weight than their flat race brothers. This form of racing does however call not only for great riding ability, but above average dash and determination.

There are also positions in a National Hunt yard for stable lads and girls, travelling lads, and head lads. These days ladies can hold National Hunt trainers' permits and jockeys' licences.

Case Studies

Clare is 19 and lives in a village in Berkshire not far from Newbury which is a major racehorse training centre. She works as a *stable lad*.

I did quite well at school in that I got nine O levels and four A levels. Unfortunately my A levels were not in the right subjects to get me a university place to read a subject that I was interested in. I have been riding since I was nine years old and I have had my own pony for a long time. When I was 13 I passed my Pony Club C+ test which is a fairly modest qualification.

On leaving school I wanted a career with horses so I went to a large residential riding school where I trained for the BHSAI exam. This was a three month course and I know the fees were fairly high, up to £100 a week. Some people manage to get grants for these courses, but not many I think. Having got my BHSAI certificate I then had to decide how I was going to earn my living. Teaching riding quite appealed to me, but I was much more keen on the riding side and schooling young horses.

A friend of mine is an apprentice jockey and I went to see him ride in a race at Salisbury. I had never been racing before and I had no idea how involved and exciting it was. It was this first visit to a racecourse that made up my mind — I wanted to be in racing.

The problem was to find a trainer who would take me on but there are several quite close to where I live. The first trainer that I tried was the one to whom my friend is apprenticed and he fortunately agreed to take me on as a stable lad. Boys or girls, you are all known as stable lads. He knew that I had been trained at a big riding school with a very good reputation and that I had passed my BHSAI so I think that he was fairly confident in my basic ability. I knew though that a racing yard would be both different and demanding.

Everyone in the yard starts work at 7 am. I have one horse to muck out and three to ride work on each day. When I arrive at the yard at seven in the morning I muck out my first horse, pick out his feet, brush him over, saddle him up, and ride him out for about an hour. It depends on his state of training, if we are galloping it may be shorter, but if we are on road work it may be longer. When I get back he is fed and put away for the morning. Some of the lads go for breakfast then but I don't. Some of us have a bit of a problem keeping our weight down so I usually just have a cup of tea. While I am riding my first lot, a man mucks out my second and third lots so all I have to do is saddle up and ride out. This takes me up until about 12.30 pm when the horses are fed and we go for lunch. It is important in a racing stable that horses are left in peace and quiet during the afternoons. Most trainers will not have any disturbance in the yard between about 1.00 and 4.00 pm.

I have the afternoon off and have to be back at work at 4.00 pm. This is when I groom all my three horses thoroughly. This is a very important part of their training. Not only does it keep them clean and free from infection but a thorough 'strapping' as we call it is like a massage. Good for the coat, skin, and muscle tone.

On race days the yard is very busy as some of the staff will be away which leaves more work for those left behind to do. There is always plenty of sweeping, mucking out and filling haynets to do, so it is quite hard work.

I get every other weekend off, that is from after lunch on Saturday until Monday morning. I am paid the same as the boys — £68 a week.

As I said the work is hard and we don't get much time off but I really enjoy it, mainly because I get so much riding on really good horses which would be difficult to find elsewhere. I'm lucky in that I have a horse of my own which I hope to bring into training at the yard in which I work. I will ride her as an amateur and when I have ridden in 15 races I will be able to apply for my B licence which will enable me to ride as an amateur against the professionals in some races.

Jack is 22 and he lives in Wiltshire. He left school when he was 16. He has four CSEs grades 1 and 2. He has progressed from apprentice jockey to a *stable jockey*.

I have always been interested in horses particularly racing. My father was very keen and he used to take me up onto the downs at Lambourn when I was very small to see the racehorses galloping. I rode a bit as a youngster because my sisters were always interested in ponies although they never had one of their own. When I first left school I thought about going into farming but I was very small and lightweight so I thought that I would not stand much of a chance there.

When I was 16½ my weight was only seven stones so I got my father to ask one of the Lambourn trainers if he would take me on as an apprentice. I went with my father for an interview with the trainer and he told us how hard it was and how only about one in ten apprentices ever got to ride in a race, and that a much smaller percentage than that were successful even if they did get a ride. He agreed to take me on three months' probation and we had to sign a contract which laid down the conditions of work, pay, time off, etc. I had to go and live in the hostel with six other lads. Four of us slept in one room and the two senior ones had rooms to themselves. It was a bit hard at first as I had never been away from home before but I soon got used to it. There was a lady housekeeper who cooked our food, did our washing, and kept the place clean.

For the first two months I just mucked out, filled haynets, and did miles of yard sweeping. This was all useful experience as during this time I got the feel of a racing stable and the rather special way of life that is lived there. Eventually I was given my first riding lesson. This took place sitting on an old horse in a loose box and being led around by the head lad. It was all very different to the riding that I had done in the past. In racing you have a *very* small saddle and you ride with the stirrups so short that you are almost kneeling on the horse's back.

As I had ridden quite a bit before I was soon capable enough to ride out on morning work and I was given a racehorse to look after. I will always remember him, he was black, 16.2 (that means his height) and ten years old. He had been good in his time and was still quite a good handicapper. I also had the trainer's hack to look after. That is the horse that the trainer uses to ride up onto the downs to watch the horses gallop in the morning. It has to be very quiet and placid, and be prepared to stand still with the trainer on him whilst all the racehorses gallop by. That sort of horse is not so easy to find.

Life was quite hard in that first year, the trainer demanded very high standards and the head lad kept us all on our toes. Any apprentice who did not pull his weight was soon moved on.

Work started at seven each morning when we mucked out all our horses, I had three to do, then we got the first lot ready. By 7.30 am we had to have our first horses brushed down, feet picked out, rugs and saddles on, out in the yard ready for work. We would lead out in a string (single file) perhaps ten of us up onto the downs behind the head lad. He would know which gallops we were to work on and he, under the trainer's instructions, would tell us exactly what work we were to do how far to go and how fast etc.

We would perhaps ride three lots like that each morning which would take us up to lunch time. We were usually ready for this having had breakfast at about 8.15 between first and second lots.

The afternoon we had free whilst the horses were resting and we had to report back to the yard at four o'clock. Then we would groom and strap our horses, feed them, and bed them down for the night.

This was the routine six days a week. We took it in turns to work every other Sunday but the horses did not go out on Sundays.

After I had been there about a year the trainer came into the yard one morning with the owner of a very nice three-year-old colt we had in training. He told me that he had agreed with the owner that I should ride the horse in a six furlong maiden race for apprentices in August.

I couldn't believe my luck, everyone else in the yard was very envious because we all knew that he was a really good horse. I had to work quite hard to get down to the required weight and I still have to diet very strictly and go running every evening to keep my weight down.

We were second in that race beaten only by the favourite and we started outsiders at 10 to 1 so the owner, trainer, and I were all very pleased.

I have ridden a lot of winners in the five years since then and I am now stable jockey to my original trainer. He is a very good trainer and he looks after me well so I am quite happy here.

Racing is a life that you have to get used to, it's a bit old fashioned in some ways. For instance you are expected to touch your cap to the owners and their wives and the trainer first thing in the morning. The trainer, his wife, owners, the starter, the clerk of the scales, and the stewards are all 'Sir' or 'Madam' as the case may be. It is a tradition of racing and I think that it is a good thing, there is a lot that could go wrong in this sport if those in authority did not keep it fairly well under control.

It is a very specialised sort of life, long hours, a lot of travelling, and hard work. But I am doing well at it now and I do not think that I could change it for anything else.

Hunting

In spite of the strong hunting lobby and the efforts of a vociferous few, hunting is as popular and successful in the United Kingdom now as it ever was. There are numerous packs of hounds throughout the country that hunt regularly and employ a staff of what are known as 'hunt servants'. These people are the permanent, paid staff who look after the kennels and horses and hunt the hounds on the day of the meet. The most senior of these is the huntsman. He is responsible for the hounds and will hunt them on the day. He may have a staff to help him at the kennels and hunt stables. There may be 15 or 20 couples of hounds to keep fed, exercised, and well. The hunt staff may have six or more horses to enable them to do their work on hunting days. In addition to the huntsman there may be one or two 'whippers in' who work in the kennels/stables during the week and play a very important part in hunting the hounds on hunting days.

Whilst the hunting season lasts from November until about the end of March, there is much to do for the hunt staff during the summer. Out of season the horses are usually turned out to grass for a rest, but the hounds have to be kept fed and exercised. The breeding of new hounds is important and it is during the summer months that hound and puppy shows are held.

The advantages of life in hunt service are numerous for those who enjoy country life and fresh air. Whilst pay is usually modest, a house is almost always provided for the huntsman and often for other members of staff. The reason for this is that with so many animals involved it is necessary to have the staff close at hand. Riding and working clothes are provided, and the huntsman and whips are often generously looked after by grateful members of the hunt.

Finding work with a hunt may not always be easy. Usually the staff employed in the kennels come from a hunting or country background, but this would not in any way exclude a person from the town who was really keen on this type of work. Whilst most professional huntsmen are men there are several very good lady 'whippers in' and the kennel and stable staff are often girls.

Promotion to huntsman is usually through the route of kennelman, whipper in and then, for the select few, to huntsman.

This post calls for a lot of experience and dedication. The ability to ride competently across country is important, but above all a knowledge of the countryside in general, and a particular knowledge of his own hunting country is vital to the good huntsman.

For those who are interested in a career in hunting a letter to the local master of fox hounds and a visit to the local hunt kennels will be the most fruitful approach. It is however another job, like many with animals, that calls for long hours, often in foul weather, strong dedication to the job, and small financial rewards. The job satisfaction though is usually high.

Chapter 4

Farriers and Blacksmiths

Farriery

For many hundreds of years man has been protecting the horse's feet by nailing onto them a narrow band of iron. Whilst many attempts have been made to improve on this technique — glued on plastic shoes, strapped on leather shoes — none has ever replaced the original method. It is with the art/craft of shoeing horses that the farrier is involved.

Horses are shod for three main reasons.

1. For protection; the horse's foot grows and is worn down perfectly satisfactorily under normal circumstances, but the extra strain that we put upon the horse by riding him or using him to pull a cart puts extra wear and tear on the feet.

2. For grip; rather like the studs in a football boot, horse shoes, the nails, and sometimes the studs that we put in the shoes provide extra grip for hunting, jumping, or for the mounted policeman riding on the tarmac road.

3. For surgical reasons; there is an old saying 'No foot no horse', and it is a very true saying. The horse's feet often become damaged as he is ridden. This can result in corns, bruised soles, damage to the horn of the foot, injured tendons, damaged joints, and many other problems. Often the combined effort of the veterinary surgeon and the farrier can relieve or cure these problems. Better still, with good shoeing they can prevent the condition arising at all.

Good shoeing can add to the horse's comfort, well being, and efficiency. Poor shoeing or neglect of the feet can cause the horse great discomfort, and in the worst cases render him useless as a working horse. There are some instances where horses can be ridden or worked without shoes, but in general all horses in serious work are shod. The farrier and his craft play a major part in all the activities of the horse world, so much so in fact that much of what we do with horses would be impossible without the farriery profession.

The farrier must not only be a skilled craftsman, able to make and nail on a shoe. He must be able to weld, sometimes make his own tools, have a detailed knowledge of the horse's conformation particularly the foot, joints, muscles, bones, and tendons. He must have a knowledge of the correct stance of the horse and his basic paces, walk, trot, and canter. Above all he must be patient, sympathetic, and understanding. Short temper or an irritable nature are not suitable attributes for a farrier. He must have a true interest in and affinity with horses if he is to be successful.

Qualifications and Training

Farriery is such a skilled and important job that it is necessary to be registered before you can practice. This registration can only be achieved by serving a four year apprenticeship with a master farrier. Candidates do not need any formal educational qualifications, but a good standard of education is always useful. At the end of this four year apprenticeship you are required to take the diploma examination of the Worshipful Company of Farriers. If you are successful in this examination you qualify as a registered shoeing smith, (RSS). This entitles you to set up in business as a farrier on your own, should you wish to.

To carry out this apprenticeship you must first find a master farrier who will take you on. If you have trouble finding a master your school's careers officer or CoSIRA (see p. 92) may be able to help you. When you have found a master you should apply to the Worshipful Company of Farriers, Field Officer, 58 Hall Park Drive, West Park, Lytham, Lancashire for an apprenticeship application form.

Under the Worshipful Company's apprentice scheme you will receive a weekly wage which should increase as your training progresses. You may also be eligible for a grant from the Company for books, tools, and clothing. You are required as an apprentice to attend a farriery course once a year at one of the Company's recognised training centres. These centres will be notified to you by the Worshipful Company.

Once you are a qualified RSS this need not be the end of your formal qualifications as a farrier. With further study and experience you can take the Worshipful Company's examination to become an associate of the Farriery Company of London (AFCL) and eventually become a fellow of the Worshipful Company of Farriers (FWCF). When you have obtained the RSS diploma you are qualified, with the approval of the Worshipful Company, to take on and train apprentices yourself under the Company scheme.

Working Conditions

The demand for skilled farriers is very high, and most farriers have much more work than they can cope with during a normal working day. This means that often farriers work very long hours. The farrier is traditionally a very strong man, but physical strength is not sufficient in itself. Farriers will tell you that backache is an occupational hazard, as so much bending down is required. Developing the knack of picking up a horse's foot and using the tools is very important, much more so than sheer physical strength.

Most farriers work from a forge where people bring their horses to be shod; this is the workshop in which a horse can stand whilst he is being shod. It contains the farrier's fire, anvil, and tools. More and more farriers now travel to their horses to shoe them. Many have a small landrover type vehicle with a mini gas forge and an anvil in the back. As most horse shoes these days are machine made, the farrier can take a supply of ready made shoes in the truck with him, select an appropriate set, make the necessary adjustment in his portable forge, and shoe the horse perfectly satisfactorily in this way.

Some farriers will 'cold shoe', that is make a ready made shoe fit without heating it. This is usually less satisfactory than hot shoeing, but when done by an expert can be adequate.

Blacksmithing

The blacksmith's trade is similar to that of the farrier but the term blacksmith usually implies that he is also involved in other iron work and agricultural engineering. This should not detract in any way from his skill as a shoer of horses. In fact the terms farrier and blacksmith are largely interchangeable as far as the layman is concerned.

Case Study

Tom is 22 and has just got his RSS certificate. He lives and works in Buckinghamshire as a *farrier/blacksmith*.

When I was small there was a blacksmith's shop in the village, and it was always popular with the children who would go down there to see the horses and watch the blacksmith at work. I spent a lot of time there and looking back I think it was the noise and the smell that fascinated me. The smell of burning hoof is very characteristic, and I always liked the ring of the big hammer on the anvil.

At school I was interested in engineering, motor cars really, and I wanted to work in a garage when I left. As there were no garages near me where I could get an apprenticeship I thought that the next best thing would be to try to be a blacksmith. By this time the forge in my village had closed down, but a new master farrier had opened up in the next village to us. I went to see him and he told me that he was qualified to take on an apprentice for training but that I would have to register as an apprentice with the Worshipful Company of Farriers. I did this, and he agreed to take me on trial for a month.

At first I just did odd jobs to get the feel of the place, sweeping, making the tea, holding horses, and fetching and carrying but I learnt a lot about what happens in the forge during this period. After a bit I went onto how to remove a worn shoe. I learnt how to light the fire and keep it going, I also learnt all about the blacksmith's tools and their use.

A lot of the work we did away from the forge. My boss had a landrover with a small gas forge in the back and we would go off for the day round the various stables, and regular customers that had phoned and asked him to come. He knew the size of the horse's feet and had a set of shoes ready for most of his regular customers. It only then needed a little adjustment when we got there. At first I would remove the shoes and he would trim the horse's feet and nail on the new shoes. Sometimes all that was needed was a trimming of the foot and the old shoe was good enough to put back on. Often we would go to the local riding school where we would do about ten horses and ponies and be there all morning.

Most horses and ponies are very good at being shod but some that have been badly handled or mistreated can be a bit difficult. If you are firm but quiet with them they usually come round in the end.

When I had been doing this for about a year, I started on preparing the foot with the rasp and the knife, and was soon able to nail on the shoe. This is where you have to be really careful as there is only a very narrow part of the foot where you can drive the nail and if you go wrong you can cause a lot of damage.

We used mainly machine made shoes that come ready made in various sizes. You have to make a slight adjustment to them to get them to fit a particular foot. Sometimes you can do this cold but hot shoeing is really better as you can get a much better fit. One of the most important things you learn as a blacksmith is that you must make the shoe to fit the foot and not the foot to fit the shoe!

In my second and third years I started making special shoes in the forge. This was a real challenge and I enjoyed it a lot. I must admit that I wasted quite a lot of iron before I made a shoe that could be allowed anywhere near a horse's foot. Often the local vet would come in to ask for some special shoe to be made, or to ask for the master blacksmith's advice on some particular problem regarding a horse's foot. From these discussions I learnt a lot about the structure of the foot and the horse in general.

There were times when we got involved in things other than shoeing horses. Often in harvest time a local farmer would come in with a piece of broken combine harvester or some other machinery that needed a quick welding job. This wasn't very popular, but I never knew him refuse a local farmer who was in a race against the weather.

During my apprenticeship I had to go off on some short

courses for training. These were mainly to teach more about the technical and theoretical side of the job, and I learnt quite a lot.

I got a small grant from the Worshipful Company which paid for my farrier's apron, books, and some tools, but my boss made me make my own pincers, pritchel, and buffer. These are small tools that the blacksmith uses all the time.

At the end of four years I took my exams and passed, but I have stayed at the same place as there is plenty of work for two of us and my boss is thinking of taking on another apprentice. My pay as an apprentice was not very good, although it did go up as I became more skilled. Now I get good money and I can easily average £100 a week, more if I care to take on more work. There is plenty to do around here for skilled blacksmiths and it seems to increase all the time.

Chapter 5

The Services

The King's Troop Royal Horse Artillery

The King's Troop Royal Horse Artillery is stationed at St John's Wood, London. Its duties as part of the household troops include the firing of royal salutes in Hyde Park on royal anniversaries and state occasions, and providing a gun carriage team of black horses for state and military funerals. It also takes part on other state ceremonial occasions such as Armistace Day, the Lord Mayor's Show and the Queen's Birthday Parade. The Troop also performs the duty of the Queen's life guard at Whitehall for a month each autumn.

His Majesty King George VI expressed the wish that it should be known as the King's Troop, and upon his death the present Queen instructed that it should keep the title established by her father.

When on parade with its guns, the Troop takes precedence over all other regiments and has the honour of parading on the right of the line. To see the King's Troop firing a salute is to view one of the most spectacular forms of ceremonial in London. Seventy-one horses take part, and the officers and soldiers wear their colourful full dress ceremonial uniform. The six guns form up in line abreast in Hyde Park and gallop into action. A salute of 41 guns is then fired and as the last round echoes across the park, the guns are hooked onto their teams of horses and they gallop away.

During the summer the Troop performs a musical drive at the Royal Tournament, and at the various agricultural shows and military tattoos up and down the country. It is an exciting and spectacular display of horsemanship carried out at the gallop, culminating in the dangerous scissor movement when the teams cross in the centre of the arena with no visible gap between them.

The Troop has 111 horses and they are nearly all Irish. The majority arrive as five year olds and are trained at St John's Wood. Some arrive unbroken so the training is always varied, interesting, and rewarding work. Part of the horses' military training includes being taught to jump. Therefore, when they have satisfactorily taken their places on parade, those showing promise are further trained to take part in jumping competitions. Many well known international competition riders have come from the King's Troop. Soldiers who show an interest and ability are encouraged to take part in various military and civilian competitions.

Soldiers joining the Troop can either serve as mounted soldiers, or as saddlers, farriers, clerks, tailors, storemen vehicle drivers, or batmen, but everyone learns to ride.

Training

Those who work with horses are all given riding instruction and those who do well are trained both on parade and on the musical drive in their first year. Those with less ability may take a season or two to learn, or may become limber gunners or stablemen responsible for feeding the horses. They all get a chance to ride out on exercise in the morning and each man is allotted his own horses to look after in the stables. Although some knowledge of horses and riding is desirable before joining, this is not essential. The main requirements are keenness to learn and willingness to work the long hours necessary when working with animals.

Potential recruits for the Troop are given a week's trial at St John's Wood before they join the Army to see if they are suitable. If they are accepted they then do the normal basic training course at the Royal Artillery Depot at Woolwich before joining the Troop.

Full details can be obtained from any local Army careers information office.

The Mounted Dutyman in the Household Cavalry

Since the second world war, and the final departure of the horse in favour of mechanisation, a composite regiment known as the Household Cavalry Regiment, based at Hyde Park Barracks, has been found to carry out public duties whilst the two service regiments of the Household Cavalry, the Life Guards and the Blues and Royals, are deployed worldwide on normal armoured or armoured reconnaissance tasks. The Household Cavalry Regiment consists of two sabre squadrons, the Life Guards Squadron, and the Blues and Royals Squadron. The Regiment is commanded by a lieutenant colonel and with its 260 horses its task is to carry out the traditional role of the Household Cavalry. Each day it finds the Queen's life guard at Horse Guards, the official entrance to Buckingham Palace, all escorts and certain dismounted duties for the royal family and visiting heads of state.

To ensure the maintenance of military standards within the Household Cavalry all officers and soldiers, with the exception of specialists like farriers, saddlers and riding instructors, are required to do periods of mounted duty and periods with the tank or armoured car squadrons.

Training

All recruits to the Household Cavalry carry out their basic training for 20 weeks at the Guards Depot, Pirbright. On joining they state their preference for mounted or mechanised duty. Those selected for mounted duty, on completion of basic training, are posted to London where they form a ride for mounted training.

The mounted training course is for 20 weeks. In this time the trooper is trained from a complete beginner to becoming a fully qualified mounted dutyman class 3, capable of taking his place on ceremonial duties. He is trained through a gradual but sustained progression of confidence-building exercises on horseback, instruction in horse management and horsemanship, simple veterinary problems, and how to clean, fit and wear saddlery and uniform.

During the first 16 weeks recruits ride exclusively in khaki. As almost all recruits join as non-riders the time is spent developing fitness and riding ability.

On the first day the recruits are introduced to the horse and are taught how to saddle up and lead in hand. Emphasis is placed on the importance of quiet handling and how to approach a horse. In the first week they are taught how to mount and dismount, and how to ask the horse to go from halt to walk and trot, and back again to walk and halt.

By the third week they are cantering and have mastered most of the riding school movements. In the fourth week they are riding for one and a half hours a day. In the fifth and sixth week they start jumping and learn to ride without saddles. At the end of the eighth week they ride the 25 miles from London to Windsor where they spend the next eight weeks of their mounted training.

At Windsor they are able to concentrate on the mounted training which includes learning to ride in full ceremonial uniform and carrying a sword.

Much hard work, sweat, and possibly tears go into graduating from recruit to mounted dutyman. The training is a steady progression, and nobody is overpaced. If the riding staff feel that a man is falling behind, he is put back a ride so that he can catch up. The man who is ahead of his ride through superior fitness or riding ability may well be moved forward a ride. Everybody without exception, from lieutenant colonel to trooper, has to go through riding school on arrival at the Household Cavalry Regiment.

Full details of pay and terms of service can be obtained from the local Army careers and information office or from: The Careers Office, The Household Cavalry Regiment, Combermere Barracks, Windsor, Berkshire SL4 3DN.

The Mounted Police

The modern Police Force is equipped with every technical device available from computers to helicopters to assist it in the fight against crime. There are however several tasks which the policeman can still do better from horseback. These tasks are ceremonial duties, escorts, and crowd control, as well as normal police duties on the beat.

The Metropolitan Police have 200 horses stationed in and around London. Their training centre is at Imber Court near Esher in Surrey, and they have mounted detachments at New Scotland Yard, Bow, Epsom, Hammersmith, Vauxhall, and Hyde Park. The City of London Police also have a mounted section.

Training

To become a mounted policeman one must first train as a normal policeman and complete the six months basic training course at Hendon. On successful completion of that course the probationer policeman completes a tour of duty at a local police station as a constable on the beat. At the end of 18 months to two years he is eligible to apply for special duty, eg as a mounted policeman, and if his record is satisfactory his application will be considered.

For those who wish to become mounted policemen, if they are successful at the selection interview, they will attend a six months riding and horsemastership course at Imber Court. Many officers who apply have no riding experience, and the course starts with the basic principles. The training includes riding, care of the stabled horse in all respects, and the specialist riding and police duties required of the mounted policeman. At the end of the course the successful students are posted to a mounted station where once again they are on probation, and will for some months work generally in the stable, getting the feel of mounted police duties, grooming, tack cleaning, and riding most of the horses. Once a probationer has proved himself he will be allotted a horse and will become a mounted police constable.

He will of course be eligible for all the benefits that the police force offers, good pay, pension scheme, and housing allowance etc.

Eventually the most capable mounted police constables are posted to Imber Court, where they become responsible for training recruits to the mounted branch, and for training young horses up to the standard where they can safely carry an officer on mounted duty.

The following police forces have mounted branches:

> The Metropolitan Police
> The City of London Police
> Ther Merseyside Police
> The Lancashire Police
> The Yorkshire and Humberside Police
> The Nottinghamshire Police
> The Staffordshire Police
> The Sussex Police
> The West Midlands Police
> The Greater Manchester Police
> The Avon and Somerset Police.

Whilst the qualifications to join the police force vary a little from force to force, a recruit is usually required to meet the following requirements:

To be at least 5ft 8ins (172cms) tall (males) 5ft 4ins (162cms) (females), some police forces have a small number of mounted women police officers.

To have perfect eyesight without aids of any kind.

To be physically fit and in good health.

To have four passes at GCE O level or CSE grade 1, to include English language or mathematics, or to pass an entrance examination standard throughout the forces of England and Wales.

To be of good character.

Full details of a career in the police force can be obtained from any major police station, or from *Careers in the Police Force* by Jean Joss and published by Kogan Page.

Mounted Duty with the Royal Corps of Military Police

The Royal Corps of Military Police carry out for the Army exactly the same duties as the civilian police forces carry out in civil life; law enforcement, traffic control, security, escort, and protection of VIPs etc.

To enable the Military Police to perform their duties they have a number of mounted policemen. This unit is stationed at Aldershot in Hampshire where they have 21 horses.

Their duties include patrolling the ranges and training areas, ceremonial escort for royalty and other important people, other ceremonial duties, a mounted display of 'tent pegging' with horses and motor cycles at major shows and displays, under certain circumstances patrolling the royal parks in London, and of course other normal police duties.

Once a recruit to the Royal Corps of Military Police has completed his basic military training at the regimental depot at Chichester in Sussex, he is posted for his first tour of duty in a field force unit. This could be in the UK, Germany, Northern Ireland or in any other military station. Having completed his first tour of duty as a military policeman, he may then apply to be trained as a mounted military policeman. If he is selected he will be taught to ride at Aldershot by the Royal Corps of Military Police riding instructors, and on completion of his training he will start mounted duties. His mounted training will include care of the horse, horsemastership, and stable management.

For further, up to date information with regard to pay, terms of service etc, you should apply to your local Army careers information office, the address and telephone number of which may be found in the telephone directory.

Case Study

Michael is 24 and he lives in Surrey. He is at present with the *mounted police* in the London area.

I left school at 16 with four GCEs and without really knowing what I wanted to do. The school's career officer was very helpful and I considered many possibilities. A career with horses was certainly not one of them. The only time I had come into contact with a horse was on a pony trekking holiday in the Lake District when I was at school.

Up until the age of 22 I had several jobs, I worked in a shop, in a restaurant, and in an advertising agency. None of these offered me any scope for adventure, or the hope of working anywhere other than indoors.

One summer at a large agricultural show I saw the police information and careers tent which looked very interesting. I had a long talk with the careers officer there who was very helpful, and told me about all the various opportunities that were available to a policeman after he has completed his basic training and a probationary period on the beat. At this stage I had still not considered the mounted branch.

A career as a policeman appealed to me so I completed all the application forms, and after two to three weeks I was interviewed and given a written examination which was quite searching but not really difficult.

After another month or so I was accepted and went off to do my six months basic training course. This was hard both physically and mentally. The standards were high and we were kept under pressure. But I think that it was only to be expected. When I passed my course I was posted to a station where we worked closely with the mounted branch. As I worked with them I became more and more interested in horses and started to take riding lessons at a local riding school.

At the end of my first two years I applied for training as a mounted police officer, and after more interviews I was accepted and sent off to start my mounted course. As a good number of the students on the course had never ridden before everything started at square one. This was good because the police style of riding was quite different to that which one would learn in a civilian riding school. The basic principles are similar, but the riding requirements of a mounted policeman are very different to those of the everyday rider.

The course lasted for six months. Besides riding we learnt horsemastership, stable management, veterinary care of the horse, and of course all the special duties that a mounted policeman and his horse are required to carry out. We did a lot of riding school work and drill riding, but we also did a lot of jumping, mounted skill at arms, riding and jumping without saddles, and a lot of work riding our horses in mock demonstrations, riots and crowd control duties when the police horse has to be so steady and sure.

When I passed out from my mounted course I was posted to a station that had a mounted section. Here for the first few months I was what we call a 'uniformed strapper'. That means that I was a mounted police constable but I was employed mainly on the dirty work mucking out, cleaning tack and equipment, sweeping etc. I did however ride most of the horses in our section. Soon I was allotted a horse and was on full mounted duty. She was a very good police horse, a grey mare called Bella 16.2½ hands high, a 14 year old, and a very experienced animal.

My first job was with three other officers on crowd control at a football match, but fortunately everyone was very well behaved and there was no trouble on my introduction to mounted duty. Since then I have been on escort duty for VIPs, general beat duties, several demonstrations, and many football matches.

I think that horses are very good for the police, it may seem an old fashioned method but the public like them. I have made a lot of friends both young and old whilst on mounted duty. They all want to pat and stroke her and give her tit-bits. Somehow she is a good introduction for me to the public and the people I have to deal with.

Having horses of course creates extra work, tack and boots to clean, mucking out, feeding and grooming. You cannot just put your horse away in the garage for the week-end for someone else to service like a motor car, but I don't think that many of us in the mounted branch would swap with our colleagues in the traffic branch.

Chapter 6

Breeding and Stud Management

Introduction

This is one of the most important areas of the whole horse world. Without efficient studs and horse breeders, quality horses would not be available for the various equestrian activities. It is therefore important that young people are trained correctly to carry on this vital profession.

To be able to work in this field one must be proficient in:

- ☐ Handling stallions
- ☐ Care of brood mares
- ☐ Care of foals and young stock
- ☐ Covering mares
- ☐ Veterinary care, particularly with regard to pregnancy and parturition
- ☐ General stable management and horse mastership
- ☐ Grassland management.

Several studs in the British Isles provide courses of training in this work. They are broadly divided into those which breed ponies or light horses and those which breed thoroughbreds. A list of those breeding ponies can be obtained from the National Pony Society, and those breeding thoroughbreds from the Thoroughbred Breeders' Association.

As well as the skills listed above, it is a great advantage to be a competent rider particularly if you are a light weight. Pony studs always need good, small, lightweight, riders for backing young ponies, and thoroughbred studs need good, lightweight, but not necessarily small, riders for backing young thoroughbreds. Really skilled and sympathetic riders are very necessary in this area of the horse world.

To make a complete study of breeding a foal takes at least a year; it takes about 11 months from conception to birth. This means that most stud courses last either from spring to spring or for periods approximately covering late spring/early summer one year and a similar period the next in order to cover the complete cycle.

Training

The National Pony Society provides two highly respected qualifications for those who are intent on serious careers in stud management and breeding. These are:

The diploma in pony mastership and breeding, and
The stud assistant's certificate.

The syllabus for the diploma states that, 'It is intended that the possession of this diploma should be a guarantee of a high standard of knowledge and ability in pony mastership and breeding'.

At least three years' experience at an approved stud is necessary for all candidates and they must have attained 21 years in order to take the examination.

No academic qualifications are required, but it must surely be an advantage to have at least O level English and perhaps even biology.

The examination includes:

Part 1 — Breeding. Covering, foaling, weaning, the handling of pony stallions, brood mares, and foals. Some physiology and the care of the 'in foal' mare.

Part 2 — Breaking. Leading, lungeing, backing, handling, fitting, and use of tack.

Part 3 — Pony Stable Management. Fodder and feeding, watering, bedding, grooming, exercise, clipping, the foot and shoeing, saddlery and its care, and extensive veterinary knowledge.

Part 4 — Show Production and Presentation. The ability

to turn out all types of pony to show standard. The transportation of ponies.

Part 5 — Riding. Riding a number of horses and ponies to show active and efficient horsemanship. Be able to jump well and have a knowledge of basic dressage movements. Have a sound knowledge of all tack and its fitting.

Part 6 — Agricultural Management of Studland. Grassland management, fencing and gates, poisonous plants, water, fertilisers, soil testing, drainage, stable layout, and design.

The syllabus for the stud assistant's certificate lays out similar aims to those of the diploma but it is set at a slightly lower level. Candidates are required to be at least 17 years of age and to have had at least one year's experience in a reputable stud.

The examination is once again divided into a number of parts:

Part 1 — Breeding
Part 2 — Breaking
Part 3 — Pony/Stable Management
Part 4 — Show Production and Presentation
Part 5 — Riding.

The requirements of each of these parts are similar to those of the diploma examination but they are set at a lower level.

Full details of these examinations may be obtained from the National Pony Society (see p. 91).

Whilst these qualifications are designed for pony studs, the basic principles also apply to studs that breed horses. Apart from part of the BHSI examination, there are no formal qualifications dealing with the skills that are required to work in a stud that breeds horses. It would obviously be an advantage to anyone who was applying for a post on a thoroughbred stud to hold a National Pony Society certificate.

For those who are considering a career in horse or pony breeding on their own, it should be remembered that all stallions must be licensed. This law is however at present under review.

Chapter 7
The Horse Trade

Introduction

To cope with the 'explosion' in horse sport and the general interest in horse riding, driving, and showing, there has been a similar 'explosion' in the associated horse trades, saddlery, riding clothes, horse feeds, horse books, prefabricated stables and buildings, all weather riding surfaces, etc. It will be seen from this by no means exhaustive list that a large number of skills and trades are required in the manufacturing, wholesale, retail, distribution, and advertising world to provide the goods required by the riding public. This requirement must provide career prospects for those interested in horses and their related activities.

Many saddlers, riding clothes manufacturers, equestrian bookshops, etc besides having permanent retail shops have mobile trade stands which they take to horse shows and horse trials to show and sell their goods to the horse public at places where its members can be found in large numbers. The trade stand areas at the Badminton and Burghley Horse Trials and at the Horse of the Year Show at Wembley each year are very popular with the visiting public and do a very good trade. These trade stands have to be transported, erected, and manned by staff who are knowledgeable in the horse world, and who can converse and deal with the horse public intelligently and efficiently.

Compound horse feeds (horse cubes) are being developed and marketed more and more. The trade is very competitive as many brands are available. There are clearly good career opportunities in horse nutrition and the marketing of horse feeds for those who have both an interest in the horse and sales or development.

As livery costs increase, and more horses are kept in urban and suburban areas, the popularity of prefabricated, wooden loose boxes, tack rooms, and feed rooms also increases. To design, construct, and market these buildings requires not only a knowledge of building design, carpentry, and sales but a knowledge of horsemastership, stable management, and the requirements of the horse world.

This is not an exhaustive list of the areas in the 'horse trade' where careers are available for people with an interest in horses. It does indicate however, that there are many opportunities to combine one's interest in horses with some other trade or skill in order to find a rewarding and satisfying career.

The only trade that offers formal training is that of the saddler.

Training

The Cordwainers Technical College

Rural Saddler's Course

A cordwainer was originally a shoemaker: he derived his name from the high quality leather that was imported from Spain in the middle ages. This leather was called cordwane, hence the craftsman's name. Today the name only refers to the guild.

The Cordwainers Company is one of the oldest in the City of London, having been granted its first ordinances in 1272. The Company now runs the Cordwainers Technical College in Mare Street, London (see p. 95) which, amongst other things, runs a craft course in rural saddlery.

The course. This is a one year full-time course which can be taken by suitably qualified young men and women.

The objectives. To widen the practical ability and to improve the skill and technical knowledge of the saddlery apprentice, or of those people concerned with horses and riding.

Entry requirements. Candidates must be 18 years or under if apprenticed to a master saddler. All candidates must satisfy the principal and head of department that they have the aptitude and will benefit from the course.

Duration. The course commences in September and finishes in July of the following year.

Fees. These will be notified by the college on application. Additional expenses will be incurred by students needing to live away from home. Students are encouraged to buy all tack and other products made during the course, provided that it is judged to be of a satisfactory standard.

Content. The syllabus is designed to introduce students to all aspects of the work which the rural saddler is likely to meet. The work covers both the practical and the required technology under the following headings: bridle work, saddle work, harness work, and riding boot repairs.

Qualifications. Students are prepared for the CGLI craft certificate examination in rural saddlery.

Grants and awards. Since this is a recognised course full-time students normally resident in the United Kingdom may be elegible for a local education authority scholarship award. Information on this should be obtained from the student's own local education authority. (The telephone number is in the directory under County Council.)

The Worshipful Company of Loriners (spur makers) awards two bursaries to the highest exam passes in lorinary, and a certificate to all saddlery students who pass their exam in bits and bitting. The Worshipful Company of Saddlers awards two bursaries and certificates to the highest exam passes in bridles and saddlery.

Case Studies

Marion is a *sales lady* who works in a retail saddler's shop.

I have always been interested in horses and ponies, and up until the age of 16 I had my own pony and was a member of the Pony Club. I used to attend all the rallies and went to pony club camp each year. I passed the Pony Club B test when I was 15½. What I really liked was competition jumping, and I would have liked very much to have been a horse trials rider. At 16 I had outgrown my pony, and he was getting a bit old for competition jumping. We still have him, and he is over 20 now and retired. I could see that I was never going to be able to compete on horses, as it was all so expensive and I had to go out to work to earn my living. When I left school I had two O levels and two CSEs so I had some academic background but not that much.

I took a job in a boutique selling clothes, as I thought that I was quite interested in fashion, but that soon became rather dull. I moved to another shop where we were given training in sales techniques and the retail trade in general. I became very interested in this, and soon became head of a small department in the big store and learnt about buying and stock control etc. All this time I still had a real interest in horses and, whilst I was not riding, I went to all the shows and followed all the show jumping competitions very closely. As I took the *Horse and Hound* every week I always looked down the 'situations vacant' column just in case there was something that would suit me. One week a large firm of saddlers and riding clothes retailers advertised for an experienced retail salesperson, who had a knowledge of horses and saddlery, to work in their shop in the Midlands, and to travel with their trade stand to shows and horse trials. This sounded exactly like me, so I applied for the job, was interviewed in London, and was successful. I think I was appointed because of my B test and pony club background and my three years' experience in the retail trade.

I am only an assistant at the moment, but I think that there is every chance of promotion, as the saddlery and riding clothes business is booming. So now at 21 I have a job that I really enjoy, I go to all the big shows and events, I meet a lot of people in the horse world, I am paid about £80 a week, my expenses are quite good when I am away at a show and have to live away from home. There is a rumour going round that the firm is going to take a stand at the big international equestrian trade fair in Germany next year, so we are all looking forward to a trip out there.

Simon is 24, he lives in Warwickshire, and he studied agriculture at college on an ordinary national diploma course. He now works as an *animal feed* salesman.

I rode quite a lot when I was at school and when I was at college, mostly on other people's horses. I rode in a few point to points and would have liked to have been a national hunt jockey but I got much too heavy. I could only just make 12 stone 7 pounds with my saddle for point to pointing, so I had no chance at all for getting down any lighter for racing under rules. When I left college I looked for a job with horses in which I could use my college training, but I could find nothing that involved riding or working directly with horses.

One week I saw in *The Farmer's Weekly* an advertisement put in by one of the major animal feed manufacturers who wanted a salesman in their horse feeds division. As the advertisement said that a car would be provided as well as a salary I decided to apply. Several of us were interviewed, some with the same agricultural diploma as me. I got the job mainly, I think, because of my fairly wide experience of horses which the others did not have.

Now I travel round to all sorts of stables, racing stables, hunt stables, livery yards, riding schools, show jumping yards, and several private stables. I often go to shows with our trade stand, and sometimes we give talks to riding or pony clubs on horse feeding and nutrition.

I have been offered quite a lot of riding from the people I meet on my rounds, and I hope that I might even get the offer of a ride in some point to points if I can get myself fit enough.

My pay is over £5,000 a year and I am provided with a car. The hours are fairly long, I do a lot of driving, and I am away from home quite a lot. The work is interesting and I am trying to find a way to return to college some time to study animal nutrition in more depth. I think that there is plenty to do in the horse world with regard to nutrition. There is room to make it more efficient and cheaper. So I think that I have found an interesting and useful career with horses.

Chapter 8

Horse Welfare Organisations

The Royal Society for the Prevention of Cruelty to Animals

The use of the horse in the service of Man, either in sport or as a working animal, lays him open to abuse and misuse, not just by the unscrupulous, but also by the ignorant. As horse sports become more popular and horse riding spreads more into the urban areas, the risk of the horse being misused increases.

There are a number of welfare organisations, some charities and some largely voluntary, who look after the horse's interests in cases where he might be subjected to misuse.

Perhaps the largest of these is the Royal Society for the Prevention of Cruelty to Animals (RSPCA). Whilst this society is concerned with all animals, it has a particular interest in the horse as he is so vulnerable compared with other animals. The RSPCA takes a particular interest in horse shows and horse trials, horse sales, abatoirs where horses are slaughtered, horse-drawn caravans, rodeos and jousting tournaments, transport of horses by land, sea, and air, and the export of live horses and ponies for slaughter. To do this, the Society trains a number of inspectors who watch over the horse's interests in the above circumstances. They give helpful advice and make reports where necessary. Whilst the RSPCA does bring some prosecutions under the law, its main interest is to help and educate, rather than to report or prosecute.

Training

From time to time the Society runs training courses for inspectors. On these courses, the trainees are taught to wear the Society's uniform and to be diplomatic representatives of the Society in public. They are given a broad training to include all animals, and receive particular information about horses. They visit a number of important horse organisations, and equine training establishments.

Places on these courses are open to both men and women and applicants must be between 20 and 35 years of age. No particular academic qualifications are required but a good general education is expected. Most of all the Society is looking for a person with a sense of responsibility, an interest in animal welfare, smart appearance, and the ability to act with diplomacy. Full details of these courses can be obtained from the Royal Society for the Prevention of Cruelty to Animals see p. 94).

Homes of Rest

A horse's working life may last up to 15 or even 20 years, depending on his type and the work in which he is involved. His life span, though, can be up to 30 years or more. It is a widely held view that when a horse comes to the end of his useful working life he should be destroyed, as it is uneconomical to keep him, and that to turn him out to grass only results in deterioration and suffering. The contrary view is that the retired horse should be turned away to grass in comfortable retirement as a reward for services rendered. The latter course is expensive and requires considerable supervision if it is to be successful.

To provide these retirement facilities a number of homes of rest for horses exist. These are:

The Ada Cole Memorial Stables Ltd
The Bransby Home of Rest for Horses
The Home of Rest for Horses.

Their addresses are all listed on p. 94.

71

Whilst no formal training of a specialist nature is given for these organisations, qualified grooms and nurses are from time to time required.

For those who feel that their careers may be with retired horses, a letter to one of these organisations, enclosing a stamped addressed envelope for a reply, may prove fruitful.

Chapter 9

Other Careers

Journalism and Photography

No journalist or photographer is handed a job on a plate. Like an artist, sculptor or song writer you have to produce your work, sell it, and establish yourself as an expert in your chosen field.

If, however, you are interested in horses and you have any journalistic flair, perhaps you were good at and liked writing essays at school, you may be able to make a career as an equestrian journalist.

Perhaps the best way to go about this is to go to your local horse show and to write a report on one or two of the main classes. This should only be short to start with, covering the main points, making a feature of any point of particular interest (perhaps the winner was a young local rider), and giving the results. Your report should be factual, interesting, informative, and grammatical. This could then be sent to your local newspaper who may show an interest.

A report of this type will surely be enhanced by a good black and white photograph. Photographic equipment is very inexpensive these days, and the camera that you would require to take this sort of photograph is obtainable fairly cheaply.

The normal 35mm SLR with a shutter speed up to 500th of a second is ideal. With this you will need a telephoto or telephoto zoom lens for taking close up shots at a distance. If you have a telephoto lens you can manage with a 135mm lens to start with. If you can afford a telephoto zoom lens an 80-210mm lens will be very suitable.

The next refinement, that is very useful for taking

pictures of horses in motion, is an auto winder. This is a device that winds on the film in your camera automatically allowing you to take shots in quick succession without having to turn the film on manually.

The best film to start with is a black and white 400 ASA film. This is a fast film that will give you the best opportunity of getting a good picture in poor light, and will enable you to use high shutter speeds when the light is good.

Your local photographic dealer will always be pleased to help and advise you on cameras, lenses, films, and equipment if you explain to him exactly what it is that you are trying to do.

It should be stressed that this is *not* a ready made career, but all journalists and photographers have to start somewhere. If you are sufficiently determined and dedicated there is no reason why you should not succeed. Further information can be obtained by sending a stamped, addressed envelope to: The Photographic Careers Centre, Southey House, 320 Croydon Road, Beckenham, Kent.

Veterinary Work with Horses

The huge increase in the horse population and in competition riding over the past few years has created a considerable demand for equine veterinary care. This has led to an increased number of veterinary surgeons specialising in horse care. Before becoming an equine vet, however, it is necessary first to train in general animal care.

The careers of veterinary surgeon and animal nursing auxiliary, which involves working with a veterinary surgeon, are described in detail in *Careers Working with Animals* published by Kogan Page.

Chapter 10

Applying for a Job

Most jobs that are advertised ask one to apply in the first instance in writing. As this will be the first contact that the applicant has with the potential employer, it is important to make a good impression. The correct way to write such a letter is taught in most schools but if one is in doubt about how to do this a careers master, teacher, parent, vicar, or local social worker will usually be pleased to help and advise. The advertisement may well ask for brief personal details and experience, or a curriculum vitae as it is sometimes called. It is worth preparing this with some care as an employer will almost certainly be impressed by a short but clear and well written c.v.

If called for an interview, you should be on time and look presentable. The horse world is still one in which neat and tidy clothes are important. They need not be expensive but should certainly be clean and appropriate. Training shoes are not good when working with horses and other clothes should be suitable for the job. Unusual clothes for men, beards, long hair, or ear rings may not appeal to the average horse owner, racing trainer, head groom, or riding school owner.

Punctuality is important, if you are going to be late for some reason telephone and let the employer know. It is only good manners to do so and may help to create a good impression.

Before attending for an interview find out whether or not riding clothes should be taken. Often, for a job working with horses a candidate is required to ride at an interview.

It is a mistake to take on a job as a 'stop gap' until

something more suitable turns up. It is unfair to the employer and may not look good at a subsequent interview.

At the interview make sure that the following points are covered (it does no harm to make a few notes to remind you what to ask about).

- ☐ What are the exact duties of this job?
- ☐ Is it a permanent job?
- ☐ What are the weekly working hours?
- ☐ Is overtime paid or is time given off in lieu of extra hours worked?
- ☐ What days of the week are leave days?
- ☐ Holidays?
- ☐ Fringe benefits ie riding lessons or other training, working clothes, hunting, competing, keep of own horse, accommodation, food, transport — use of car. These are often given in lieu of some pay, so it is important to discuss what happens if you start off with some of these fringe benefits but they are discontinued later.
- ☐ National insurance contributions — if you are earning more than £28.50 per week you are required to pay these contributions so that you are entitled to sickness and unemployment benefit.
- ☐ Insurance — riding is a high risk occupation, what cover is provided for employees who are injured during the course of their duties?
- ☐ What are the wages? When are they reviewed? Is one paid weekly or monthly? How, by cheque or cash? Is an itemised pay slip provided with the wages (it should be)?
- ☐ Ask to see the accommodation, if any is to be provided.
- ☐ Ask to see the stables and the horses.
- ☐ Ask to meet other members of the staff, if any.
- ☐ What are the terms of giving notice to quit on either side?
- ☐ Who is to be your direct superior?
- ☐ Is there a probationary period to start with? If so for how long?

☐ Is a contract provided (it should be, by law after 13 weeks employment)? It is better to get one in writing after a month though, if possible. It should contain:

Name and address of employer and employee
Job description
Date employment starts
Wages and method of payment
Hours of work
Fringe benefits
Holiday entitlement, holiday pay, public holidays, and holiday situation on termination of employment
Pay during sickness or injury
Pension, if any
Notice of termination of employment for both employer and employee. (It is in the interest of both the employer and employee that this contract is correctly drawn up at the very latest by the thirteenth week of employment.)

Part 2

Chapter 11

Full-Time Courses in Various Equestrian Studies

Full-Time Courses in Various Equestrian Studies

There are a number of colleges, agricultural colleges, technical colleges, and colleges of further education that run full-time courses in various equestrian studies. These colleges are broadly spread across the United Kingdom.

The major advantage of attending one of these courses is not only that one receives a very thorough training, but that the chances of obtaining a local authority grant are considerably better if one is attending a course at a college that is accepted by the education authorities, than if one is attending a course at a riding school. However, sometimes grants are made for students to train at riding schools.

The courses available (June 1982) are as follows:

Carmarthen Technical and Agricultural College (in association with The British Horse Society), Carmarthen SA31 2NH
A course in equine studies (1 year)

A course in equine studies

This course leads to the following qualifications:

1. BHS assistant instructor's certificate.
2. Certificate in equine studies awarded by the college under the technical supervision of the BHS.

Course content
Students will receive theoretical and practical training in:

Equitation
Stable management and horsemastership
Horse ailments and treatment
Riding instructional techniques.

The successful completion of examinations in these subjects will lead to the award of the BHS assistant instructor's certificate.

Further equine and business studies will include the following subjects:

Equine sports and national bodies
Breeding and stud work
Equine nutrition
Equine industries
Business organisation
Banking and financial services
Office practice.

Students will spend the autumn and summer terms at the Carmarthen Agricultural and Technical College and the spring term at the British Equestrian Centre, Kenilworth, Warwickshire.

Entry requirements
GCE O level passes (or CSE grade 1) in at least four subjects to include English language or literature.
Proficiency in riding to approximately Pony Club B test standard.
Satisfactory completion of college and BHS selection interview.
Minimum age 17 years on 1st September prior to the commencement of the course.

Newark Technical College, Chauntry Park, Newark
Course to prepare for the BHS assistant instructor's certificate (1 year); the BHS assistant instructor's examination and business studies (2 years); the BHS intermediate instructor's course (36 weeks)

1. The assistant instructor's one-year course

This is a full-time intensive course in preparation for the BHSAI certificate.

Course content
> BHSAI subjects (see two-year course)
> Elective studies
> Liberal studies
> Complementary studies (eg financial management, typing, business management)

Entry requirements
> As for the two-year course.
> To be 16 years and 10 months of age at the date of entry to the course.

2. The assistant instructor's two-year course

This is a full-time course commencing each September, designed to meet the needs of those students who wish to train for a professional career with horses. The BHSAI examination will be taken during the course, together with examinations for the Riding Club and Pony Club certificates.

Course content
> Equitation
> Stable management, theory and practice
> Basic veterinary work
> Instruction work

Other studies undertaken with this course are chosen from:
> GCE O level subjects
> GCE A level subjects
> Secretarial studies ie typing, shorthand, book keeping, etc.
> Business studies (BEC certificate)

Entry requirements
Four or more GCE O levels (or CSE equivalents) one of which must be English language or literature.
Pony Club B test or equivalent or be able to demonstrate sufficient riding ability.
Satisfactory completion of interview and tests.
Minimum age of entry 16 years.

3. The BHS intermediate instructor's course

This 36-week full-time course commences in September and finishes at the end of June. It gives complete training in all aspects of the BHS intermediate instructor's and horse knowledge and riding stage IV certificates.

Other subjects included on this course are:
  Business and financial management
  Speech and voice production
  First aid
  A full range of evening studies in A and O level subjects
    is available if required.

Entry requirements
Applications must hold the full BHSAI certificate, and have at least one year's riding teaching experience since passing that examination.
Successful completion of interview and tests.
Two referees who will vouch for the applicant's riding and teaching ability.
  Financial assistance may be available for all these courses. Applicants should apply to their local education authority.

North Tyneside College of Further Education
Embleton Avenue, Wallsend, Tyne and Weir NE28 9LL
Equestrian and business studies course.

Equestrian and business studies course

This is a two-year full-time course commencing in September, designed to meet the needs of those students who wish to train for a career with horses.

The following examinations are taken during the course:

1. The British Horse Society certificate of horse-mastership.
2. The British Horse Society preliminary teaching test.

Course content

Equitation
Stable management and horsemastership
Minor ailments
Lungeing, riding, and leading
Taking a class lesson
Giving clear explanations of lesson subjects and teaching formats
Giving novice leading rein and lunge lessons
Giving lecturettes
Safety and first aid

3. Business Education Council national certificate

Course content

People and communication
Numeracy and accounting
The organisation in its environment
Quantitative accounting methods
Administration in business
Business law

Entry requirements

☐ Four GCE O level subjects at grades A, B or C (or CSE grade 1), or a BEC general award at credit level. English language or literature is necessary in order to take the BHS preliminary teaching test.
☐ Applicants should possess either the Pony Club B certificate or be able to demonstrate relevant potential.
☐ Satisfactory completion of interview and tests.

☐ Minimum age of entry to the two-year course, 16 years.

The Warwickshire College of Agriculture Moreton Morrell Hall, Moreton Morell, Warwick CU35 9BL. The certificate in horse management course (1 year); the ordinary national diploma in horse management (3 years); the equine studies, business management and intermediate instructor's course (35 weeks)

1. The certificate in horse management course

This course concentrates on the care of horses with special reference to stud work, young horse development and training, and horses in relationship to land use. It is intended for those people who wish to make a career in horse management either on their own account, or as a key person in a larger establishment or farm.

Candidates have a choice of two options within the course depending on whether they intend to make their careers in teaching or non-teaching establishments. The former group have the opportunity to enter for the BHSAI certificate and the latter for the Royal Society of Arts certificates in typewriting skills and office practice.

Course content
(a)   Horse and stable management
        The horse
        Stable management
        Stud management
        Schooling
        Riding
(b)   Agriculture
        Animal husbandry
        Crop husbandry
        Grassland management
        Machinery
        Estate maintenance
        Stud and stable office work

(c)   General studies
(d)   Teaching option to certificate
       Equitation up to BHS certificate of horsemastership level
       Teaching up to BHS preliminary teaching test level
(e)   Office practice option to certificate
       Office routine, typing, etc

This one-year, full-time, residential course leads to the Warwickshire College of Agriculture certificate in horse management, plus, for those following the teaching option, the BHSAI certificate and, for those following the non-teaching option, the Royal Society of Arts certificate in typewriting and office practice stage 1 (stage 2 also for suitable candidates).

Entry requirements

To be at least 17½ years of age on 1st September in the year of entry to the course.

To have at least one full year working with horses.

To hold the Pony Club B test, Riding Clubs grade 3 test or BHS horse riding and knowledge certificate stage 3.

Candidates for the teaching option must hold four O level certificates or their CSE equivalents, one of which must be in English language or literature.

Candidates for the non-teaching option must have a good general education up to GCE O level standard.

2. The ordinary national diploma in horse management course

This course is intended for students who have ambitions to own their own equine establishments, or seek employment as stud and stable managers. The aim is to give an understanding and appreciation of the fundamental scientific principles of stable and stud management; the related aspects of agriculture coupled with sound training in practical skills, and to familiarise students with appropriate planning techniques and systems of business control, together with the staffing and running of a commercial equine enterprise.

The objectives are, that at the end of the course, participants should have sufficient knowledge to enable them to carry out the majority of day-to-day tasks associated with stable and stud management and the related farming enterprises, and be capable of employing a large range of planning skills in a variety of horse and relevant agricultural situations.

After a further period of relevant practical experience it is expected that participants will be capable of taking full responsibility for a horse enterprise.

Course content
1. The horse
   Role of the horse
   Anatomy and physiology
   Conformation
   Veterinary science
   Schooling
   Stables and ancillary buildings
   Nutrition and grazing management
   Stud management
   Equitation
2. Agriculture
   Animal production
   Grassland management
   Crop husbandry
   Machinery
   Estate maintenance
3. Business management
   Records, accounts and office routine
   Legal and economic aspects
   Business management

This is a three-year course starting in September each year. It is a sandwich course, years one and three being spent at the college and the second year being spent away at one or more equine establishments to gain practical experience.

At the end of the course successful candidates will be awarded the ordinary national diploma in horse management.

Students with the appropriate qualifications will also be entered for the BHS stable manager's certificate.

Entry requirements

To be at least 17½ years of age on 1st September in the year of entry to the course.

To have a minimum of one year's full-time practical experience working with horses.

To have four GCE O levels (or equivalent) including two science subjects and preferably English language.

To have one of the following qualifications:

BHS certificate in horsemastership.

Irish certificate in equitation science.

BHS horse knowledge and riding certificate stage 3.

Pony Club B test.

BHS riding club grade 3 certificate.

NPS certificate in pony mastership and breeding for stud assistants.

3. The equine studies, business management and intermediate instructor's course

This course caters for those people who have already proved their aptitude and interest in their chosen career of riding instructor, and who now require further education and training. The aim is to give a basic understanding and appreciation of the fundamental principles of stable management, and the necessary practical and theoretical education and training in equitation, teaching, schooling, horse management, and office practice. This is to enable course members to pass the BHS intermediate instructor's certificate, general certificate in education, and Royal Society of Arts examination in selected subjects related to office and business organisation.

It also aims to broaden the students' outlook and to assist in their personal and general educational development.

The objective is to produce people with sufficient background knowledge and practical skill to enable them to carry out the majority of day-to-day tasks associated with an equitation centre and who, with further relevant practical experience and training, will be capable of becoming BHS instructors and successfully running a riding or training establishment.

Course content
>Horse management
>Equitation
>Teaching
>Equine development
>Stud farm management
>Business studies
>General studies

The course is a full-time non-residential course of 35 weeks, divided into three terms and starting each year in September.

Successful candidates will be awarded:

☐ The Warwickshire College of Agriculture certificate in equestrian business management

☐ The British Horse Society intermediate instructor's certificate.

In addition students will also have the opportunity to enter for:

The Royal Society of Arts certificate in office practice (stage 2)

GCE O level in book keeping and accounts.

Entry requirements
>To be at least 18 years of age on 1st September in the year of entry to the course.
>To have had a minimum of one year full-time working with horses.
>To have either at least four GCE O levels (or equivalent) including English, or an appropriate college certificate

in horse management. (Candidates over 20 years of age may be exempted from some of these academic entry requirements.)

To hold the BHSAI certificate.

To demonstrate during a practical test that they have 'flair and feel' as riders.

Potential students are reminded that courses in any field of education are, of necessity, constantly under review. This results in changes being made from time to time in course content, entry requirements, duration of course, etc. Be sure to apply to the college of your choice for the up-to-date syllabus.

Grants are sometimes available to help with fees, accommodation, and travel. If you think that you would qualify for a grant you should apply to the office of your local education authority. Their address will be in the telephone directory under 'county council.'

The Worcestershire College of Agriculture Hindlip, Worcester WR3 8SS

Certificate in stud and stable husbandry (6 weeks)

Certificate in stud and stable husbandry

This course is for people who are already working with or who are connected with horses, and are firmly committed to working (dismounted) with horses.

Age is not important and no specific qualifications are required, however applicants will be required to provide evidence of some success in formal studies.

The course is of six weeks' duration, taken in three separate blocks of two weeks. It is held between October and May.

Course content
   Conformation
   The skeleton
   Feeding and digestion
   The blood system and respiration

Reproduction
Health and hygiene
Housing
Stable routine
Grassland
Vehicles and other equipment

Useful Names and Addresses

The following addresses may be useful to you if you wish to find out more about any particular aspect of the horse world. Remember that it often helps to enclose a stamped, self addressed envelope with your enquiry if you want a quick reply.

Breeding and Stud Management

The Hunter's Improvement and National Light Horse Breeding Society, 8 Market Square, Westerham, Kent TN16 1AW

The National Foaling Bank, Meretown Stud, Newport, Shropshire

The National Pony Society, Cross and Pillory Lane, Alton, Hampshire

Equestrian Sports Societies

The British Driving Society, 10 Marley Avenue, New Milton, Hampshire BH25 5LJ

The British Horse Society, Stoneleigh, Kenilworth, Warwickshire CV8 2LR

The British Show Jumping Association, Stoneleigh, Kenilworth, Warwickshire CV8 2LR

The British Show Pony Society, The Croft House, East Road, Oundle, Peterborough

The Ladies' Side Saddle Association, Wykham Lodge, Jubilee Drive, Upper Colwall, Malvern, Worcestershire

The Western Horseman's Association of Great Britain, The Poplars, Wisbech St Mary, Cambridge

Farriers and Blacksmiths

The Council for Small Industries in Rural Areas, 141 Castle Street, Salisbury, Wiltshire

The National Master Farriers', Blacksmiths' and Agricultural, Engineers' Association, 674 Leeds Road, Lofthouse Gate, Wakefield, Yorkshire

The Worshipful Company of Farriers, 3 Hamilton Road, Cockfosters, Barnet, Hertfordshire EN4 9EH

Heavy Horses

The British Percheron Society, Owen Webb House, Gresham Road, Cambridge CB1 2ER

The Clydesdale Horse Society of Great Britain, 22 Argyle Terrace, Dunblane, Perthshire

The Heavy Horse Preservation Society, The Old Rectory, Whitchurch, Shropshire SY13 1LF

The Irish Draught Horse Society of Great Britain, North Brook End Farm, Steeple Morden, Royston, Hertfordshire

The Shire Horse Society, East of England Show Ground, Peterborough PE2 0XE

The Suffolk Horse Society, 6 Church Street, Woodbridge, Suffolk

Horse and Pony Societies and Associations

Angus
The Secretary, The Shetland Pony and Stud-Book Society, 8 Whinfield Road, Montrose, Angus DD10 8SA

Berkshire
The Secretary, The Lusitana Breed Society, Hillfields Stud Farm, Lower Basildon, Berkshire

Buckinghamshire
The Secretary, The British Trakehner Association, Buckwood, Fulmer, Buckinghamshire

Cleveland
The Secretary, The Dales Pony Society, Ivy Farm House, Hilton, Yarm, Cleveland

Cumbria
The Secretary, The Fell Pony Society, Packway, Windermere, Cumbria

Dorset
The Secretary, The British Spotted Pony Society, Wantsley Farm, Broad Windsor, Beaminster, Dorset DT8 3PT

The Secretary, The Dartmoor Pony Society, Weston Manor, Corscombe, Dorchester, Dorset DT2 0PB

Dyfed
The Secretary, The Welsh Pony and Cob Society, 6 Chalybeate Street, Aberstwyth, Dyfed SY23 1HS

Galway
The Secretary, The Connemara Pony Breeders Society, 73 Dalysfort Road, Salthill, Galway, Ireland

Gloucester
The Secretary, The British Appoloosa Society, Ash Cottage, Icomb, Stow on the Wold, Gloucester GL54 1JO

Hampshire
The Secretary, The New Forest Pony Society, Beacon Corner, Burley, Ringwood, Hampshire BH24 4EW

Leicestershire
The Secretary, The British Quarter Horse Association, Hyline Stud, Holly Farm, Madbourne, Market Harborough, Leicestershire LE16 8DX

London
The Secretary, The British Morgan Horse Society, George and Dragon Hall, Mary Place, London W11

Oxford
The Secretary, The English Connemara Society, Buttermilk Farm, Leafield, Oxford OX8 5PL

Perthshire
The Secretary, The Highland Pony Society, Wester Sunnyside, Methuen, Perthshire PH1 3RF

Shropshire
The Secretary, The Caspian Pony Stud (UK) and Society, Hopstone Lea, Claverley, Shropshire

Somerset
The Exmoor Pony Society, Quarry Cottage, Sampford Brett, Williton, Somerset

Sussex
The Secretary, The Arab Horse Society, Sackville Lodge, Lye Green, Crowborough, Sussex

Warwickshire
The Secretary, The Hackney Horse Society, The British Equestrian Centre, Kenilworth, Warwickshire CV8 2LR

West Midlands
The Secretary, The Hafflinger Society of Great Britain, PO Box 8, Ettingshall, Wolverhampton, West Midlands WV4 6JP

Wiltshire
The Secretary, The British Palomino Society, Cholderton, Salisbury, Wiltshire SP4 0DX

Worcestershire
The Secretary, The Donkey Breed Society, Manor Farm Cottage, Buckland, Broadway, Worcestershire WRL2 7LY

York
The Secretary, The Cleveland Bay Horse Society, York Livestock Centre, Murton, York YO1 3UF

Horse Welfare Organisations

The Ada Cole Memorial Stables Ltd, 2 Gleneagle Road, London SW16

Bransby Home of Rest for Horses, Bransby, Saxilby, Lincoln LN1 2PH

The Home of Rest for Horses, Westcroft Stables, Speen Farm, Aylesbury, Buckinghamshire HP17 0PP

The International League for the Protection of Horses, 67a Camden High Street, London NW1

The Royal Society for the Prevention of Cruelty to Animals, The Causeway, Horsham, Sussex

Hunting

The British Field Sports Society, 59 Kennington Road, London SE1 7PZ

The Master of Foxhounds Association, Parsloes Cottage, Bagendon, Cirencester, Gloucestershire

Veterinary Organisations

The British Equine Veterinary Association, Park Lodge, Bells Yew Green Road, Frant, Tunbridge Wells, Kent TN3 9EB

The British Veterinary Association, 7 Mansfield Street, Portland Place, London W1M 0AT

The People's Dispensary for Sick Animals, PDSA House, 21-37 South Street, Dorking, Surrey

The Royal College of Veterinary Surgeons, 321 Belgrave Square, London SW1 8QP

Others

The Apprentice Training School, Goodwood House Stables, Chichester, Sussex

The Association of British Riding Schools, 7 Deer Park Road, Sawtry, Huntingdon, Cambridgeshire PE17 5TT

The British Equestrian Trades Association, Wothersome Grange, Nr Wetherby, West Yorkshire LS23 6LY

The Careers and Occupational Information Centre, Manpower Services Commission, Moorfoot, Sheffield SW1 4PQ.

The Cordwainers Technical College, 182 Mare Street, Hackney, London E8 3RE

The Horse Race Betting Levy Board, 17/23 Southampton Road, London WC2

The Jockey Club, 42 Portman Square, London W1H 0EN

National Association of Grooms, PO Box 7, Tetbury, Gloucestershire

Riding for the Disabled Association, Avenue 'R', The National Agricultural Centre, Stoneleigh, Kenilworth, Warwickshire CV8 2LZ

The Race Horse Owners' Association, 42 Portman Square, London W1H 9FF

The Racing Information Bureau, 42 Portmand Square London W1

The Society of Master Saddlers, 9 St Thomas Street, London SE1

Weatherby and Son, 42 Portman Square, London W1

The Worshipful Company of Loriners, 2-5 Benjamin Street, London EC1M 5QL

The Worshipful Company of Saddlers, Saddlers Hall, Gutter Lane, Cheapside, London EC2V 6BR

Chapter 13

Reading List

This list of books will help those who are seriously studying for a career with horses. They can usually be obtained from the local public library. If they are not held in stock the librarian will, in most cases, be able to make a special order.

For grooms
Rose, Mary FBHS (1950) *The Horseman's Notebook*. Harrap
Hayes, Capt M Horace FRCVS (1968) *Veterinary Notes for Horse Owners*. Stanley Paul

For instructors
As for grooms plus:
The British Horse Society (1968) *The Instructor's Handbook*
Crossley, Anthony (1978) *Training the Young Horse*. Stanley Paul
Inderwick, Sheila (1977) *Lungeing the Horse and Rider*. David and Charles
Podhajsky, Alois (1973) *The Riding Teacher*. Harrap
Podajsky, Alois (1967) *The Complete Training of Horse and Rider*. Harrap
Sivewright, Mrs RCT FIH, FBHS (1979) *Thinking Riding*. J A Allen
Mortimer, Monty (1981) *The Riding Instructor's Handbook*. David and Charles

For breeding and stud management
Andrist, F. (1966) *Mares, Foals and Foaling*. J A Allen
Wynmalen, Henry (1971) *Horse Breeding and Stud Management*. J A Allen

For saddlers
Edwards, E Hartley (1971) *Saddlery*. J A Allen
Tuke, Diana (1969) *Bit by Bit*. J A Allen
Tuke, Diana (1970) *Stitch by Stitch*. J A Allen

In the event of these books being difficult to obtain, they can all be purchased from: The British Horse Society Book and Gift Shop, Stoneleigh, Kenilworth, Warwickshire CV8 2LR.